To Andree Gronback,
- a good friend
and neighbor,

With Appreciation,
Earl F. Lindsay

One Incredible Journey

a clergy person's calling

Earl F. Lindsay

AuthorHouse™
1663 Liberty Drive
Bloomington, IN 47403
www.authorhouse.com
Phone: 1-800-839-8640

First published by AuthorHouse 7/12/2010

ISBN: 978-1-4520-3039-5 (e)
ISBN: 978-1-4520-3037-1 (sc)
ISBN: 978-1-4520-3038-8 (hc)

Library of Congress Control Number: 2010907650

Printed in the United States of America
Bloomington, Indiana

This book is printed on acid-free paper.

"I have called you by name
You are mine!"

DEDICATED

To my father, Frank Herbert Lindsay, who taught Sunday School until he was 86 and to my mother, Violet Mary Lindsay, who could make a delicious meal out of practically nothing!

FORWARD

When Earl asked me to write a few words about his new book, I was both humbled and pleased. I want you to know that I have not yet read the book nor do I know just what it is about, BUT, I do know Earl F. Lindsay and what he is all about! This is why I can with complete confidence recommend that everyone read this book.

Earl was born and raised in a small border town between North Dakota and Minnesota. His parents were of modest means but with a real Christian set of values. It's no wonder that Earl chose to go to Vennard, a small co-ed private school in Chicago, with a strong religious overtone. It was there that Earl met the love of a lifetime---his wonderful Eleanor and they began their life together, a life of full time service to Jesus Christ.

Earl worked hard and did well enough to be accepted at Garrett Biblical Institute on the Northwestern campus. With hard work and the devotion of his life partner, Earl handled many student changes and eventually became ordained an Elder in the Methodist Church. Years later, while serving a large Wisconsin Church he undertook and achieved the Doctor of Ministry Degree from San Francisco Theological Seminary.

Earl recognized early in his ministry that the important thing was the local church because without the local church being strong and creating value for its members and community, there would be little or no need for all of the FRILLS of the conference and it's many varied councils and boards.

Earl clearly understood what Harold Washington Ruopp was describing when he said: "Great ministers don't stand on the River Bank of Life shouting commands to their parishioners---they jump down off that River Bank of Life and into the swim---putting their arms around us and saying---Come on, together we will make it". And so it has been with this exceptional minister. He has always been in the swim of life with us. For that, along with many other things, makes countless hundreds of Methodists across Wisconsin grateful for his having been here and serving our local churches. If, as I assume, this book tells the story of the journey of this amazing man and his devoted wife, Eleanor, I assure you, you need to read this book and get acquainted with Earl.

Steven J. Rosing,
Layman and business executive
Portage, Wisconsin

Every pastor needs a friend like Steve Rosing. He recognizes your achievements, offers honest evaluation, listens as you describe your frustrations and cares about your total family!

Who could ask for anyone more? EFL

PREFACE

In my high school years, I was one of the fastest 100 yard dash runners in my school. In such a short run I could give it my all and it was over so quickly. I have a little of the same feeling as I complete over 60 years of ministry. It has been a fast paced life and frankly, I thrive under those conditions. For me the ministry has never been a job—mere employment; it has always been a calling------not something I entered because it was one of many choices, but, somehow I could do no other! And , to think, I was paid to do what brought such immense fulfillment. Who could ask for anything more?

This short trip through "clergy-land" has included a wide collection of friends, the best in education, Worldwide travel, and the deep down feeling that the God who cared for me in my youth is even closer to me in these later years. To paraphrase the late Professor Albert Outler of Southern Methodist University, "Our God doesn't call all the shots, but does share all of the blows"! –and at all ages!

I am grateful for a biblical faith experience that began with my parents and a little Methodist Church in the Dakotas. That faith was both tested and expanded by the wonderful people who worshipped at Perrinton and New Buffalo, Michigan, Madison First, Portage, Whitewater, West Allis First, and Kenosha First, in Wisconsin.

There were clergy like Fred Hill, Carl Wesley Stromberg, Winslow Wilson, Gordon Amphlett, and Stanford Strosahl who formed my style of ministry and were friends who were always there. There were also church members like Roy and Helen Murray, Steve and Clarice Rosing, Chester and Kathy Dickow, Charles and Bonnie Graham, Sharon and David Rumachik, Eldon and June Rinka, and George Affeldt who were "pillars of support" in these years of service. No statement of appreciation would be enough, however, for the best friend I ever had, in clergy-land or anywhere else, my wife of 60 years—Eleanor C. Lindsay. I thank God for her most of all, and also our daughter, Joy, three sons: Mark, Paul and Michael, their spouses, our nine grandchildren and six great-grandchildren. They have provided both challenge and immense joy (plus a whole lot of illustrations).

Earl F. Lindsay, author

PREPARATION FOR THE JOURNEY

When I was a Freshman in College, I heard this hymn. It was written by the late Professor Kenneth B. Wells. It has been ringing in my heart and in my head from that day until today.

"Called of God to build his church,
with Christ himself the cornerstone!
This our one desire to know the Christ
and make Him known.
Thanks to God for years of preparation
for His service high
To earth's remotest bounds
we take this truth we've found
And thank God for His love!"

The author's educational preparation for ministry involved 7 years of perfect attendance in Sunday School, high school diploma from Wheatland, ND, Bible diploma from Vennard College, Bachelor of Arts from Alma College, Master of Divinity from Garrett-Evangelical Theological Seminary, Doctor of Ministry from San Francisco Theological Seminary, and Post Graduate Merrill Fellow from Harvard University. Also attended Methodist Theological Seminary in Seoul, Korea and Emory University in Atlanta, Georgia.

World travel has also been a part of our preparation to minister. Over the years of our ministry, we have led 21 world tours, covering 5 continents, 61 countries and all 50 states. This has greatly expanded our understanding (and also those who have traveled with us) of world issues and better acquainted us with Biblical knowledge, historic movements and the diverse make-up of the many people who live in this universe.

CONTENTS

INTRODUCTION

The English Poet, Lord Byron, once wrote "tis pleasant to see one's name in print; a books, a book, although there is nothing in it."

I would hope that this book could have a larger purpose than simply to have "one's name in print" and as the journey of a life time unfolds it will reveal what a calling really is and how the path to and through clergyland is both stimulating, challenging and a whole lot of fun.

Henry David Thoreau once said "I require of every writer, first and last, a simple and sincere account of his (or hers) own life". In this book you will find that the story is told through one's life-time of experience.

The purpose of this book is to help those persons who are considering pastoral or professional ministry, as they weigh the merits and demerits of their decision to realize that one could never handle all that "ministry" should include; it requires the leading of the Spirit and the love and support of an entire community.

The road to and through pastoral ministry will include an abundance of mistakes, an assortment of frustrations and at times you will wish you were somewhere else, but, as one realizes that you will have a part in transforming lives and families: you will have helped society move through tremendous social changes; and you will be changed yourself.

It is also my hope that these experiences could help some pastor, who has lost his/her way, find the courage and the faith to try again! Not one of us has all the Gifts and Graces that we need, but, the Biblical incentives that have renewed my journey again and again are these two passages: the words of the Prophet Isaiah and the words of the Apostle Paul:

"I will turn the darkness before them into light, the rough places into level ground---and I will not forsake them"! Isaiah 42:16 (NRSV)

"I have strength for anything through Him who gives me power"! Philippians 4:13 (New English Bible).

James Stephen has written, "Originality does not consist in saying what no one has ever said before, but in saying exactly what you think yourself." It is in this "mind set" that I offer you "One Incredible Journey"!

CHAPTER 1
"In The Beginning"

Our early years have such an influence on the rest of our lives! When my grandparents decided to leave their Canadian home to begin a new life, they homesteaded in Dakota Territory in 1885. With their Canadian neighbors they joined a circuit rider's church (Methodist) even though they had been faithful Episcopalians all of their lives. This decision set the stage for my spiritual journey for my father married and brought my mother to that circuit (several) of churches. I was the first of six children to begin my spiritual journey in that Wheatland, ND Methodist Church. No one finds who they are or what they are for without the input of many individuals, and as Hillary Clinton once said, "It takes a community to raise a child". Our spiritual journey is shaped and formed by those with whom we live and move and have our being. The small town and rural atmosphere meant one to one relationships and small classes in school and community involvement. I can still name all of the students in my high school graduating class, and the whole community was like family. The urban world has changed those circumstances for many.

Our lives and the lives of our neighbors were all affected by the same forces of nature (floods, droughts, grasshoppers etc.). Yes, a large poor family whose "primetime" was a depression and a World War, all helped to shape my priorities. No spiritual journey comes to pass without the indelible influence of special people in your life, and for me it was, first and foremost, my parents: Frank Herbert Lindsay and Violet Mary Coffland Lindsay!!!! Neither was well educated nor did they have any unusual talents but both had found a strong vital Christian faith and both made parenting their first priority! My father was my high school Sunday School teacher. It made such a difference. They treasured the Bible, education, the community, the public schools, the local church, their family and their Irish Canadian heritage.

Oh, yes, there were other special people too-------like the farmer, Roy Murray, where I milked cows and drove a tractor at 12 years of age. Roy loved the Lord and urged me to go on to Vennard College. There was Mr. and Mrs. Mandel Hilde, my high school teachers who helped me be a better student and encouraged my public speaking and singing, and Paul Sheldon, my 4-H club leader who expanded my horizon, and my pastors, Rev. S.G. Samuelson, Rev. John Wesley Frisbee and Rev. Fred Hill. The first two helped me experience a personal faith in Jesus Christ and the last pastor even loaned me enough money so I could begin college. The love, the faith, the personal caring of all these special people sparked the desire to attempt this incredible journey. This journey entered another stage when my family tearfully accompanied me to the Greyhound Bus station and at age 17 I was on my way to an urban world. I had never experienced Chicago! From the cocoon of a loving home into the "jaws of a scary but exciting world: Goodbye Innocence"! It was the beginning of the Journey!!!!

CHAPTER 2
The Beginning of the Journey

In this new world of the big city (Chicago) I was immediately exposed to racial diversity and urban life! I knew only white people and a stop light was something new. Now there were black people and Hispanic people and an endless sea of traffic. While I had been driving since I was 10 years old, it was a frightening experience to drive a friend's car through rush hour traffic for the first time! I walked down Madison Street, wearing my big western hat, and stepping over people laying on the street, as I found my way to Chicago Evangelistic Institute. I was walking because I did not know how to board a bus or a street car and I didn't have the money for a taxi cab. My world was changing fast! For me, the rural open prairie was never to be again.

C.E.I. (Chicago Evangelistic Institute) was a small Bible College where a number of my pastors had attended and also youth from my home church. It was reassuring to still have one student from my home church on campus. He looked after me as if he were my father. That school (C.E.I.) made a crucial and permanent influence on my life.

It was there that I began to seriously wrestle with being a good academic student. High School was a social event but at CEI I had to work at academic issues, in fact, as I now look back it was more of a challenge than any other school I have experienced (including Harvard University). It was at CEI that the Bible came alive for me. It became the authority of my Christian experience. It was at CEI that my sense of calling, my feeling that the ministry was where I belonged---focused! I had considered the life of a farmer, law school, and teaching but now I was convinced that full time and professional ministry was where I should be. It was at CEI that I had the opportunity to practice ministry in hospitals and jails, and in evangelistic teams, articulating what I believed (limited as it was) and understood to be the Christian faith. After all, I was still a teen-ager and these 3 years were a time of maturing.

I have saved the most important benefit of being a student at CEI until the last: it was here that I met my wife, Eleanor. We met in the registration line when first arriving at school, but a certain amount of social experimentation took place before we really found each other. As I explained in later years, "One must do their research before one comes to a conclusion and realized what is best for them"! Near the end of our second year I knew who was best for me! Eleanor was from the Upper Peninsula of Michigan and we were in the same classes. I would never have passed Greek without her help and I would never have made it in the ministry without her lifelong love and support. When we completed Bible College we traveled to Eleanor's home town (Republic, Michigan) where we were married on June 15, 1951. To get there, however, was another experience! We both had jobs while we were in school as we were paying our own way, however, we were both broke. Finally, I went to a blood bank in Chicago and sold a pint of blood for $20.00 so I would have enough money for gas to get to the wedding! I made it! Today, I am even more conscious of the sacrifice that my large family made to be at our wedding and the sacrifice of Eleanor's family to provide a beautiful and sacred experience. Our parents cared about our future and supported us emotionally and spiritually, as we began our journey!

CHAPTER 3
The Churches, The Local Church

During my third year of college, a student friend received a letter from a Methodist District Superintendent in Michigan, inviting him to come to Michigan and serve as a student pastor. He could attend a liberal arts college and serve part-time in a student parish. My friend wasn't interested so I answered the letter.

On the day we were to be married a letter arrived at the home of Eleanor's parents informing me that I had been appointed to three churches---Perrinton, Pompeii, and Fulton Center, Michigan---and we were expected to be there in two weeks. We couldn't even find the towns on the Michigan map! My new father-in-law was really impressed---he said "my new son-in-law must be very good when they asked him to serve three churches"! Little did he realize that that was the bottom of the barrel!

We honeymooned in an Upper Peninsula cabin that belonged to Eleanor's uncle and from there we began the 600 miles journey with my 1939 Mercury (the first year Mercury was made) and a borrowed trailer, to this new parish. Since these towns were not on the map, we kept inquiring along the way until we reached south central Michigan. There we stopped at a farm house where I asked about Perrinton, MI and said I was the new pastor there, the lady said "Oh, you are our new pastor"! This 20 year old youth did not know whether to say "Yes, No or run"! "Oh, you are our pastor" sounded a little frightening! It was the first time anyone had referred to me as "Pastor". These three rural congregations, however, were much like my home church and while I didn't know much about being a pastor, I knew something about farms and farming!

The District Superintendent advised me that as a way of starting out, it would be good to visit in the homes of members as a way of getting acquainted. That proved to be an invaluable stroke of genius. I helped farmers bail hay, combine grain and pick corn. I knew how to do that, but what I didn't realize is that I was demonstrating to those wonderful people that I cared about them and respected their work. When one farmer lost an arm in a corn picker, I helped organize a group to harvest his corn and that story traveled all over.

One cannot be a pastor in a small town for very long until death steals one of your flock and you are faced with a frightening experience. How do you conduct a funeral—something I had never done! Mistakenly, I looked first to the funeral director for help! His only advice to me was "Keep it short" and when the service was complete, he said "I didn't mean that short".

In my first year, I was asked to have a funeral in a home. That was an old rural tradition that had almost stopped and it was the only "in home" funeral I ever conducted. The grieving widow in this circumstance, however, decided the burial of her husband would be about 150 miles away and she expected me to "give some words" at the gravesite. I drove my car and she rode with me. Days after this experience she approached me at church and asked me how much did she "owe me"? Being new and with no idea of what I should suggest, I simply said, "Oh, that's o.k.". She responded, "I told Bessie you aren't supposed to pay a preacher"! Oh, well, we made it on our salary of $17.00 per week from her church. Seriously, a lot of "Ministry" happens at funerals!

It was in this parish that I had my first experience at "family counseling". One morning I received a phone call from a very irritated and angry lady who said, "Can you come over here, I have had it with my husband"! When I arrived at their farm home, I met an elderly couple in their mid-eighties! He was in the barn and she was in the house! It seems that Bessie had made some tasty fruit cake and placed it in the basement to age. Fred had a little shop in the basement, and being winter time, he had time on his hands. One cold day when he was hungry, he noticed the fruit cake and decided to cut off a slice. Well, as the winter wore on, he had a few more slices and soon the entire cake had disappeared. Not wanting to reveal his theft, he cut a block of wood the same size as the fruit cake and carefully rewrapped it in the package! Near Christmas, Bessie had invited a group of friends to stop in for lunch. When she went to the basement to retrieve the fruit cake, she unwrapped it before her friends and discovered a block of wood----all hell broke loose! Yes, we saved the marriage but it was a tender spot for a long time!

The churches began to grow. I was learning to be a pastor and it was very fulfilling! Because I was so young (age 20) and I had lots of energy, youth ministry became our focus. We organized roller skating parties and traveled to church colleges with the High School youth. I taught history in the local high school and drove a school bus (part time). On Wednesday night we developed a circuit youth group (all 3 churches) so I drove our trusty Studebaker 20-25 miles each Wednesday picking up youth for the gatherings. My understanding and rapport with youth was expanding. During this three year pastorate, I completed my Bachelor's Degree at Alma College, a Presbyterian College in Alma, Michigan. Alma broadened my perspective and refined my skills. It was a good experience.

CHAPTER 4
Learning About The Itinerant Ministry

In Methodist Circles, there is an event called the Annual Conference and at that gathering all pastors are appointed for a new year of service. I was in attendance at this event when a new chapter of our life erupted. It was about over, after 4 days, and we were heading home to begin a 4th year of ministry when the District Superintendent called me aside. He said, "Earl, you need to attend Seminary and we have a two point parish near Seminary. I just feel it would be the right thing to appoint you there and you could attend Seminary at Garrett Theological Seminary in Evanston, Illinois (on the campus of Northwestern University). This meant I had one week to return to my old parish, say goodbye to some wonderful people, and move 200 miles to a new parish! We made it! At Perrinton, Pompeii, and Fulton Center I experienced crises, counseling, finding new members, youth leadership, and how to keep a congregation together—invaluable insight. I am forever indebted to those congregations.

New Buffalo and Lakeside were located on the shore of Lake Michigan with sandy beaches and in a busy urban-suburban setting. I was no longer working with mostly farmers and rural people. It was an urban blend!

The traffic was now very heavy and my introduction to these circumstances was my very first speeding ticket (but not my last)—right in front of the church! My introduction to the congregation was even more humbling: the lay leader of the congregation who had attended the annual denominational meeting and met us there, introduced me on that first Sunday morning. He said, "I would like for you to meet your new pastor. He isn't what we asked for but he is what we got"! He was right!

Because it was summer and because we wanted to get better acquainted with the congregation, we organized a picnic. A sizeable crowd turned out and there were lots of children. One of the events of entertainment for the day was a sack race. It so happened that three of the participants were pregnant women----and the very next morning all three pregnant women were in the hospital, including my wife and our first born, Joy, was one of the three new babies. What a great way to increase the Sunday School.

It was in this parish that I received my first lesson in being a parent and being a pastor at the same time. At our first Christmas program in the new parish, we were so excited because the church, including the balcony, was filled to capacity----But, it was one of those times when everything went wrong. The children didn't know their parts and the service was too long. Finally as the service was ending and I was greeting the last member of the congregation at the door of the church, I boosted my 4 month old daughter up in the air and said, "Sweetheart, at least you love me" and she burped, covering the front of my new robe with you know what! Life doesn't always happen as you plan it---even in the Lord's work. It was at New Buffalo and Lakeside that I had my first experience in fund raising---something that has to happen if you are to understand parish ministry. New Buffalo was an old rectangular building with a shed over the front door that looked like an old outhouse. The outside was sided with an artificial "brick" asphalt siding. It was awful. The inside was quite comfortable and furnished with new blonde furnishings. Because we were located at the intersection of two major highways and in the center of town, a novel idea struck me! Aluminum siding was new and the Alcoa Company was only 50 miles away in Chicago. So I wrote to them and asked if they would consider siding our church as an advertisement. I explained that we were a small struggling church but we were in a very conspicuous location. They responded by giving us the new siding and applying it. After more than 50 years that siding still looks good. It also bolstered my courage and helped me always to remember the Scriptures, "Ask and it shall be given, seek and you will find"!

It was from New Buffalo that I began my Seminary studies. We were only 3 miles from the Indiana border and about 75 miles from Seminary---Garrett Biblical Institute in Evanston, Illinois. For the next three years I commuted to seminary, often car pooling with other students who were also commuting to seminary. They, too, were serving student parishes and the 3 hour commuting time was a time to share experiences and test ideas. Life-long friendships grew out of that experience and one more life changing event: it was a very cold January day and my car pool group decided to go out to dinner on the north side of Evanston before we began the journey back to our parishes. When we arrived back at the school a phone call had come in about the time we had left for dinner and the call said, "come home quickly". Eleanor was pregnant and was due to deliver any time so I knew what the message meant. I borrowed a friend's car and drove to Michigan City, Indiana as fast (or faster) than the law would allow. I was met in the parking lot of the hospital by a Catholic Nun who announced that I was the father of a baby boy, Mark Duane Lindsay! Our neighbor and friend at the parish had rushed Eleanor to the hospital, and was already standing at the door giving out cigars! I had missed that great moment in my life but I was grateful that Eleanor was supported by the people of that wonderful parish. That is the Christian community!

It was at that parish that I learned that good deeds do not always produce good results! It was Christmas Day and all of our family had come to celebrate with us. As we sat down to eat dinner there was a knock at the door and there stood a very young mother and her small baby. The young mother said her husband had thrown them out of the car and left them in our small town, so---we took them in, found them a hotel room and in a few days found the young woman a job in a local

restaurant. We thought we had created good news out of bad news---but---it was just about 2 weeks later the restaurant owner and the hotel manager came to see me and explained "this innocent looking young woman was soliciting business at the restaurant and carrying it out at the hotel! I was now a Pimp! We live and learn! I had learned that even a good deed needs to be carefully examined and checks and balances need to be in place.

CHAPTER 5
Politics, Politics

As I was nearing graduation from seminary, one of my professors came to me and said "The Wisconsin Conference of the Methodist Church needs a director of youth ministries and I think you would be the right age to lead in that area"! When I expressed some interest, he contacted the Bishop of Wisconsin and soon I was asked to come to Madison, WI for an interview. I was accepted for the position, but now I was to learn about the unwritten politics of the church. You see, I did not first ask the Bishop of Michigan for permission to interview in Wisconsin and so when I did inform him of my interest in the Wisconsin position, he simply sent a curt note that said "I didn't know you were unhappy on our team. I wish you well in Wisconsin". O.K.! ---and then I also learned about what power an annual conference can exert! The annual conference approved the position in Wisconsin but voted no salary. So, there I was with a job, but no salary, and a wife and two children to support. When one of the committee heard what had happened, he called and asked me to become the Associate Pastor of the historic First Methodist Church in Madison, WI. I accepted and it was one of my better decisions!

First United Methodist Church, Madison, WI

CHAPTER 6
The Capital City and The University Church

Madison, Wisconsin, was so very different than anything I had ever known. It was a university community and the Capital of WI. The church was large and in the heart of the city. It included rich and poor, educated and uneducated, and one of my first responsibilities was to recruit one hundred and thirty-five Sunday School teachers in the first three months. From this Madison parish I received three gifts for ministry that were to bless and enrich my ministry for the rest of my life. The first gift was the tremendous resources of leadership. I continued to call on them regardless of where we lived and served-----people like Dr. Leigh Roberts, a Psychiatrist and Family Counselor, and other University specialists. There were also the political leaders such as the Governor of the State, the Attorney General, and the Secretary of Agriculture, all of which came to speak in churches where we were serving. The Specialist in the Medical Community also continued to be available and help us respond to human need. The second gift was learning how to work with important and talented people without being intimidated! On my very first Sunday of preaching and on nearly every Sunday morning, the Chairman of the Department of Speech at the University of WI, Dr. Winston Brembeck, sat directly in front of the pulpit, and nearly in the front row! I was age 26 and his presence intimidated me. One day I said to him, "Dr.

Brembeck, it must be hard for a person with your expertise in speech to listen to someone with my limited experience"! His reply I will always remember: He said "you know I didn't come to church to teach or learn speech, I came to worship the Lord and I need to do that with regularity---I may have a PhD in Speech but spiritually, I am a second grader"! Yes, God ministers to the wise and the foolish! I even had the honor of officiating at the funeral of Dr. Edwin Witte, the father of our American Social Security Program.

The third gift , perhaps more important than all others, was the friendship and counsel of the Senior Pastor of First Methodist Church, Dr. Carl Wesley Stromberg. Carl's understanding of the church, his sense of humor, his critique of my sermons and ministry activities. His continued friendship and the friendship of his wife, Leona, was an immeasurable gift to our lives and ministry. On a personal level it was Carl Stromberg who helped me understand the importance of a vacation for my life and ministry. Being a boy from the farm, I didn't know much about vacations, so when I was informed that I had one month's vacation each year, I didn't know what to do with so much vacation time. I am a high energy person who loves my work, so after two weeks I came back to work because I didn't know what to do with my time! Carl sent me home again! He said, "Vacation time is meant to rest your body and your spirit. It is a time to strengthen your family ties, your parenting skills and your marriage! Without them you will be less of a person and a less effective pastor." Everybody needs a friend like the Rev. Dr. Carl Wesley Stromberg. He was truly my mentor and my friend.

Serving as Associate Pastor in Madison means I was just a few blocks from the Bishop's office and he would frequently call me in to talk about a future appointment. It was in this relationship that I began to know a Bishop as a leader and friend, rather than as a symbol of power. His friendliness and counsel helped me learn how to trust the connectional system and while that was not true of every person who held the title of Bishop, it was true of H. Clifford Northcott.

CHAPTER 7
The Biggest Challenge Thus far!

One day while attending a retreat, my roommate for that occasion, proposed a startling question as we reached our room for the night. He bluntly asked me "Well, are you going to take it?" I didn't know what he meant, but he explained to me that he was being moved to a new parish and he had recommended to the Bishop that they ask me to be his replacement! Well, the Bishop had not asked me yet but in a few days he did call and asked if I would meet with a committee from the Methodist Church in Portage, WI. I was excited! It was a congregation of over 800 members in a county seat community of about 8,000 people. I was even more excited when I learned that they were discussing plans to build a new church. Little did I realize what that would entail but, at age 29, I was about to face the biggest challenge of my life.

I left Madison First, with a feeling of reluctance. Madison was such a beautiful city and the church was a congregation filled with community, state and national leaders, but in my heart I now belonged in Portage. They were about to receive the youngest pastor in their long history. As we prepared to leave Madison, I became ill with pneumonia and ended up in a local hospital. So, it was from that hospital that my wife loaded me into the back seat and our two children as well, and drove the forty miles on icy roads to arrive in Portage! Thank the Lord for a brave wife.

It was Lent (March) and so I was to lead the Lenten Service but because I still was so weak, I missed my first service in Portage. What a start! Because there were still some things that needed to be transported from Madison to Portage, we returned a few weeks later to retrieve them. A couple from the congregation accompanied us and since we were quite new to Wisconsin, they suggested that we see some new country and take a different route to Madison.

The "different route" entailed crossing the Wisconsin river by a small ferry but when we arrived at the river we discovered that the ferry didn't run in March because the river was still frozen over. What should we do? Well, this youthful pastor decided to drive across on the ice! Believe you me, that couple talked about their "river crossing" for the rest of their lives----and my driving reputation followed me to Portage!

For the first time I was in charge of a staff where "salaries for others" had to be recommended and working conditions determined. It is not the easiest place to make friends. Among the very early decisions that had to be confronted and it became one of the major decisions of my entire ministry was: "Should we build a new church or remodel the old one?" We were very crowded for classroom space and we were short of land, so, I thought it would be an easy decision!

Was I ever wrong!!!! When a congregational vote was taken as to building a new church the vote was 107 for building and 100 votes against building a new church! About that time I wished that I was somewhere else but I had just arrived. It, however, became one of the most "growing" experiences of my life. I learned diplomacy, patience, compromise, anger control and a little appreciation for long tradition-----all in one project! We did, however, get a new 17,000 square foot church built on ten acres on the north side of the city. It proved to be the way the city was moving and soon a high school and many new homes were built beyond us. While constructing the new church we held Sunday School classes in 3 different locations in the city and the attendance actually grew.

Because there were so many members who didn't want a new building I did not want to sell our old building to another church; I wanted to eliminate our old image as a church and take all of our members to a new location. We stumbled on to an ideal solution. The County (Columbia) needed a new court house and so we offered our old church to the county as a temporary court house while they built a new court house. They accepted and so for nearly one year they held court in our sanctuary on week days and we held church services there on Sunday mornings. When the new court house was completed, they tore our old church down and made a parking lot for the court house which was across the street. That eliminated our old location and provided us with a sizable amount of cash for our new church. I was also learning about property transaction and how to keep a congregation together.

At Portage I also learned about leadership in the community and how important that is to the growth of a church; interdenominational cooperation, service clubs, community services, jail ministry and hospital care! It was all important ministries. After nearly 7 years the Portage Methodist Church was well over 1,000 members and with a new beautiful edifice. I learned so much at Portage!

In the spring of my 6th year at Portage, the Bishop called to say he would like for me to consider a move to the largest congregation of our denomination in the state and serve as the second minister (they had four ministers). Still a little ill at ease with the powers of a Bishop, I answered very honestly by responding, "I will move if you want me to do so, but I don't really want to leave Portage". He responded, "If you don't really want to move, you don't need to move". I learned you could say "No" to a Bishop's request----but not for long!! In the spring of my 7th year, he called again and began the conversation by saying, "Earl, we need your leadership in one of our University churches, so I am not calling to ask your preference, but to let you know where you are needed"! I knew I couldn't turn down a second request. Eleanor and I knew the pastor of a university church who had announced he was moving so before we said "Yes or No" to the Bishop, we drove to that university community to see what we could learn! We liked what we saw and so we returned the Bishop's call and said "yes" to his request. He said "Fine, I want you to go to Whitewater, WI" which was a totally different church than we had researched---you cannot out guess a Bishop!!

CHAPTER 8
A Radical Change!

Whitewater, WI was a small town which had been almost overwhelmed by a mushrooming university (increasing from 3,000 students to 10,000 students). In our time the church was a large old building, one of the oldest in the city! It was somewhat depressing to move from a new church to a musty old building, but, one of the promises of ordination was to go where you are sent. This was the test of that promise!

It wasn't easy to leave Portage, a county seat with a small town, rural atmosphere that reflected our roots and where people had been so good to us. It was, however, time for a new church and different challenge---and what a change and challenge this new parish turned out to be.

Whitewater was also surrounded by a rich farming community. New professors, university employees and students were pouring into a town that had been retired farmers and milk plant employees. It was also the late 60's and both the Vietnam War and racial issues were flaming. I had not really faced up to those enormously volatile issues until I arrived in Whitewater.

We had developed a working relationship with a black congregation in Milwaukee as a way of learning about people of color and better understanding our own feelings. As part of that experience we decided to exchange worship leadership with the black congregation. One Sunday their pastor and choirs would come to Whitewater and one Sunday our pastor and choir would lead worship in their congregation. We were first, and nearly destroyed the relationship before it started. Racial tensions were very high when we arrived in Milwaukee. Father Groppi had just led a group of black people over what then was the "dividing line" and into white South Milwaukee just the week before. We arrived with our large all white choir and two of our leaders, Everett and Barbara White led the choir into St. James black church, with these words of greeting, "We are the Whites from Whitewater"! Those great people were actually amused and they continued to call us "the Whites from Whitewater". It was a break-through.

The congregation was growing fast and so we began with buying properties, creating new parking lots and up-dating a church building. We moved to three worship services which we identified as our "far in service" (8:00a.m. in the chapel), our "far out service" (9:00 a.m. in fellowship hall) and our more traditional service (10:45 a.m. in the main sanctuary). It helped us minister to this diverse worshiping community. After all, the congregation had 72 professors, 60 full time farmers, many many students, retired farmers and the business community. Who could ask for anything more? As we tried to face up to the issues of our day and our nation; one Christmas Eve Service described it best: the large church was packed and as I told the Christmas story, we had pictures flashing on the wall of Vietnam War scenes and people caught in poverty, I also asked a stranger to the congregation (but a friend of mine) who looked rather unkempt, to come walking down the aisle and up toward the pulpit during the sermon. I wanted to illustrate how hard it is to welcome a stranger into our midst. The congregation was shocked and the ushers tried to evict him before I could explain why it is so easy for all of us to say "there is no room in our inn"!

During these years Martin Luther King, Jr. and "Bobby" Kennedy were both assassinated, the main building on campus was destroyed by arson, and there were many marches. On one of those occasions, I stood with the Dean of Men from the university between 3,000 marching students and the National Guard. Both sides were led by a member of our congregation. I have often said that I have never been in military service but I have certainly been in combat.

It was during this pastorate and now in my late 30's that I began to feel the need for academic renewal. My life was changing and the world was changing. It was nearing the half way point of my professional career and I was feeling a need for intellectual stimulus. BUT, with a wife and 4 young children, how do you do that? After some searching, I learned of a program at Harvard University offering a scholarship and especially for mid-career persons. I applied and to my utter surprise, I was accepted as a Merrill Scholar to Harvard. I learned that my experience in the social struggles of the times was just the kind of student they were seeking. Thanks to my wonderful wife, who parented those 4 offspring, the Rev. Archie Henry, our Associate Pastor, who led the congregation while I was away, and the recommendations of good friends, I sat for a semester in the classroom of Professor Harvey Cox, Joseph Fletcher, H. Richard Niebuhr, and G. Ernest Wright. It was the most enriching fulfilling academic experiences of my lifetime.

I came back to Whitewater a renewed person and with even a stronger conviction that my place in this world is in church leadership. It did make me aware however, that I needed more tools and better training to give leadership in the church. I began to search for a degree program that would help me understands how to incorporate other professionals in the leadership of a congregation rather than be the solo leader.

I found such a program at the San Francisco Theological Seminary (the Graduate Theological Union) in California. It allowed me to remain in the pastorate and yet return to school for shorter periods of time over the next 4 years (The Doctor of Ministry). It wasn't an honorary degree or a correspondence school (with a false degree), it was an advanced degree in preparation for ministry and leadership. It was just what I wanted and needed. Whitewater continued to grow as a community (now over 10,000) and as a congregation (over 900 members). I was completing my fifth year there and enjoying a growing congregation----BUT it was not to be---

Youth group on retreat in Gulf Shores, AL

CHAPTER 9
The Urban Church

A call from the Bishop changed everything. He presented a request to become the senior pastor of a large urban congregation in a suburb of Milwaukee, WI (West Allis). I was flattered and challenged. The church had a sizable staff and the Bishop was even offering to let me have some voice in choosing an Associate Pastor! I accepted and in less than a month we were moving just 50 miles but to a very different world.

For my family this proved to be the most difficult move of our lives----and as a pastor I learned an important new lesson, namely; you are a parent even before you are a pastor! Our daughter who was entering her senior year of high school was unhappy with the move. West Allis, WI was a large older suburb and Whitewater was a small charming community. Joy did not like her new high school and missed her close friends. She wanted to return to her old high school and we were about to send her back when the unexpected happened, and it changed everything! The Captain of the football team asked her out and that problem was solved. There are some things parents cannot do but boy friend's can! (This relationship did not last very long but long enough to solve the immediate problem.)

The new location had some benefits for our family as well. First of all, we had a much bigger parsonage that just fit our needs and second, all four of our children traveled only two blocks to four different schools! They all began to find new friends and settle into their new community.

In a brand new parish there were two immediate challenges before us. The first was to get acquainted with a much larger congregation and the second challenge was to still have enough time to finish my doctoral studies. Getting acquainted received our first attention! How do you get to know 1200 members and let them know you are genuinely interested in their journey? We had a new idea! Instead of simply having a onetime gathering of maybe 200 people we decided to invite small groups to the parsonage every Sunday evening, until all had been invited. These weekly groups continued over nine months and about 800 people came. We learned about their families, their years in the church, their hobbies and their life in the community. It was a lasting investment in ministry that enriched all the rest of our years in that congregation. I almost wore my wife out that year but she enjoyed it as well.

West Allis was again so different than any congregation we had ever served. The congregation came from all over the metropolitan area, not just West Allis. The high school youth group had students from seven different high schools. While the congregation came from all over the metropolitan area, West Allis still had a clear identity as a suburban community. It had good schools, wonderful parks and many community activities. It was our first experience in a truly urban congregation. We were beginning to like the "big city" and my doctoral studies were helpful in how to work with a large staff. The unique talents that each staff member brought to the leadership team increased our effectiveness.

In the nearly seven years of ministry at West Allis, I personally learned better organizational skills such as a plan to contact every church member every year so a "one to one" relationship could be maintained. It became the largest congregation I was ever to serve---the third largest United Methodist Church in Wisconsin. During these years I completed my doctoral program, working with Dr. Richard Jones who was pastor at Whitefish Bay, WI. Our Doctoral dissertation is one of the few ever written by two people: Richard and myself. The intention of this project was to demonstrate with our research what "Team leadership in Pastoral Responsibilities" is about.

It was at West Allis that we began to develop more age group ministries. Thanks to a more adequate staff we did our best youth work and with the addition of a "youth bus", the teen age members grew fast in numbers. "Mission Trips" became a new way to teach youth about missions and with the help of youth choirs and bell choirs we developed a very effective youth program. One unusual project was a boy scout who chose for his "Eagle Award " to create a "taxi service" for church members who did not have transportation to the church services. He set up a schedule of drivers with a dispatcher for each Sunday and persons without transportation could simply call the church office and a "taxi" (a member of the congregation) would respond. This transportation system lasted more than 25 years. What a gift it was and it extended the outreach of the congregation.

Growing church needs good youth programs

A second new ministry for us was a "Senior League"---a monthly senior citizen's group. It averaged over 125 per gathering, did trips to many places and after 40 years, it is still very active.

We learned to love the Milwaukee big city atmosphere with all of its cultural and sports events but it was this congregation that was the center of our lives!

CHAPTER 10
The Downtown Church – At The Heart Of The City!

One midsummer morning after the Annual Conference had met, I was surprised to have an official visitor, my District Superintendent. I thought he might want to visit about our associate pastor but to my shock, he had come to offer me an invitation to a new congregation! It was a down town church in a city of over 100,000 and I was to follow a very popular and outstanding pastor and preacher. I was flattered and humbled but invigorated by the challenge of such an outstanding congregation. First United Methodist Church of Kenosha, WI was a massive Gothic structure with over 100 rooms and heavily in debt. My first church (Fulton Center) had only one room! Again, we would be moving with one son in the middle of high school and one son in the second grade. After prayer and consulting with the family, we decided to make the move. Kenosha would be my last pastorate! The parsonage had been given to the congregation and it was to be the most beautiful house we were ever to live in: a 3,000 square foot, English Tudor Mansion, overlooking Lake Michigan. We were a little embarrassed by its elegance. When our daughter came to visit she couldn't believe it was the Methodist Parsonage. We were to learn later that the roof leaked and the sewer backed up into the basement----but every house has its problems.

Kenosha First was one of the oldest congregations in the state, having been established in 1835. It was the first church in Kenosha and therefore, took on the unofficial role of THE church of Kenosha. Since it was located at the heart of the city the Pastors became counselor to all those who did not have a church and marriage counselor to those who didn't want their church or their pastor to know that they had problems. Personal counseling took more of my time than in any church I had ever served. It was one of the "special ministries" that goes with a "downtown" church!

Being at the heart of the city, however, exposed you to special kinds of problems. On one occasion I observed a rather small male "street person" using one of the church's telephones. From the conversation that I overheard I could tell it was a long distance phone call, so after about a half hour, I interrupted him and asked that he didn't tie the phone line up for much longer. He reacted very negatively but recovered sufficiently to ask if he could talk with me in my private study. Since that was upstairs and it was nearing 7:00 p.m., I thought perhaps we could visit long enough to calm down his irritated disposition.

He was carrying a small travel bag which he asked that I do not touch. He brought it with him to the study. In our visit he explained to me that the phone calls were to invite his friends to come to our church where they planned to have a "séance" with the devil! Again he cautioned, "do not touch my travel bag!" Of course our visit extended and extended and now it was nearing 10:00 p.m. The choir director had called my wife and told her if I didn't come home I should call the police because he had seen me go up to my office with a very strange appearing man. At 10:00 p.m. the phone rang and it was my wife asking where I was and if I was o.k. When I gave no answer (so as not to add to my guest's paranoia) she called the Chairman of the Pastoral Relations, who called the police. My wife also called the choir director and another member of the church. At near midnight there was a knock on the study door and when I answered, there were three policemen, the pastor-parish chairman, the choir director, and my son! My guest immediately prostrated himself on the floor and refused to move. Even the policemen couldn't move him! Finally, I offered meals and a hotel room and when the police backed away, he stood up, took my arm and all seven of us men transported him to a downtown hotel, where we turned him over to one elderly woman who owned the hotel! So goes life in a down-town church!

Kenosha was not a country church, a college church, a suburban church---it was truly a downtown church and that meant the opportunity to do certain ministries that are especially for a downtown setting. That not only meant more counseling but a unique opportunity to bring the rich and the poor together. We had business leaders, community leaders and professional people BUT we also had street people, the unemployed and the poorest neighborhood. We, therefore, developed a Food Pantry, helped to sponsor a Soup Kitchen, housed and fed street people and organized a community Thanksgiving Day Dinner. Our youth groups developed service projects and participated in helping remodel and repair the houses of the needy—both at home, in Appalachia and on Native American Reservations.

We organized and sponsored the first Korean Methodist Church in Wisconsin—which met in our chapel. Among the humorous events that grew out of this relationship was an occasion when our paper boy approached me when I returned from a three week vacation to report that "something very strange was happening at the parsonage while we were away"! He said, " there were people jumping in your swimming pool with their clothes on, and they were talking funny"! Well, the truth was I had given the Korean pastor permission to use our swimming pool to baptize Korean people by immersion! Misunderstandings happen---even in the church! We also organized a Hispanic congregation but helped them locate in another congregation's building.

Our most unique new ministry was made possible in cooperation with two large companies (Jockey International and Snap-On-Tools) when we helped develop and sponsor an Industrial Chaplaincy Program which eventually became independent. A weekly radio ministry was initiated to reach shut-ins and new residents and we heard from many listeners who lived from near Chicago to near Milwaukee. All of these kinds of ministry were possible because we held together in our church membership people with means and people without means. We did not allow our affluent members to flee to the suburbs but we challenged them to "stay downtown" and be a ministry to the whole city and the whole world! Of course that meant a vital local program that ministered to everybody's needs. That meant the best in music programming, like voice choirs, bell choirs, children's choirs, youth choirs, a wonderful pipe organ but also contemporary and ever changing music events. It also meant a full time youth director who was always looking for new youth and young adults. He/she led Jr. and Sr. High School groups, young adult groups, mission and fun travel groups and brought them into the worship life of the church. It meant regular pastoral visitation to keep a one to one relationship with every member and find those who were lost along the way! During our years in Kenosha we experienced some of the most difficult times of our ministry and so different than anything we had previously known. There was community frustration with the loss of the major industry (American Motors) which closed and that meant the loss of about 3,000 jobs. There was both a community crisis and a church crisis when a judge disappeared with his law firm's funds and he was also finance chairman of the congregation. There was a staff crisis when the Associate Pastor announced that he was gay and the congregation voted 200—203 to remove him from the pastorate. This was the most painful experience of our entire ministry! Ministry is never removed from crisis and imperfection but the wonderful part of it all is the most committed people rise to the challenge when pain and disappointment are present. Kenosha was my longest pastorate and frankly, I never felt more like I was "in my place" and where God wanted me to be than during those nine plus years. We loved the downtown church. In the pressures and busyness of one's schedule in a down town church, it is so important to remember that you are still a husband and father. One Christmas Eve between the second and third worship services, our youngest son called to say "Help. I am 4 miles out in the country and my Volkswagen quit running." So his father borrowed a chain to pull his ailing "beetle" back home. That is parenting and those kids are still a gift. During these years our family grew up on us! Our two sons graduated from high school and left us with an empty nest. It is a time when one again evaluates who they are and what they should be doing. It was time to take up a new challenge!!

CHAPTER 11
Is Administrative Service "My" Ministry?

So, when the Bishop asked me to become the Executive Director of the church's Foundation I faced a new dilemma: I was a local pastor---that seemed to be my calling---how could I become a finance person? Well, said the Bishop, "Your church is now debt free and when you came it was heavily in debt. You have always paid 100% of your mission pledges and apportionments, as we Methodists call it, and we need an experienced pastor to replace an outstanding leader in the conference who is retiring"! "But, Bishop, I am a local pastor" was my protest. He said, "Yes, but you are also a member of the conference and that's where the conference needs you right now""! O.K.! You can't argue with a Bishop very long---and win, so, after 9 plus years in Kenosha---- 726 new members, 281 baptisms, 490 marriages ----we prepared to move on!

As the new President and CEO of the Wisconsin United Methodist Foundation, I wasn't sure how I would be as an administrator instead of a pastor; now financial stewardship was my major emphases. It was not long before I learned that programming was still the center of it all and both the Biblical and organizational emphasis was similar.

First of all, I knew nearly all of the pastors in the state and that was the first point of familiarity. Stan Strosahl, the former foundation director, spent six months helping me get started.

Second, it was an aspect of Christian concern (stewardship) that had been really neglected and few pastors knew how to incorporate it into their ministry.

I began by changing the purpose of the foundation from simply overseeing the investment of funds for the state denomination to stewardship programming for the local congregations.

Surveys were conducted to see if local pastors would accept a monthly stewardship article to be printed in their local newsletters. A strong affirmative response was returned. Local churches were encouraged to invest their discretionary funds, gifts, building funds, money from wills and funds not intended for local budgets in a Common Fund at the foundation which paid better interest than many investments. We developed a stewardship program for local churches which I would lead, and thus 75% of the Sundays I was the preacher in some congregation. It grew in popularity until I was leading stewardship programs in other states and even other denominations. It was our most successful new program.

The investment program continued to grow also. It grew from 3.5 million dollars in 1986 to 23.0 million in 1992. Today (2009) that fund is well over 60.0 million and the foundation is self financed. The foundation gave me a broader perspective on the church's ministry since I was always traveling and participating in local congregations all over the state. It challenged me and it frightened me as I observed our best pastors at work and our worst pastors who didn't have a clue about leadership or stewardship!

While serving nearly 6 years as the President of the Conference Foundation, I also accepted the responsibility of building manager for the Denominational Headquarters. The

Foundation offices were housed in this complex and my office was back to back with our Bishop's office. One day the elevator wouldn't work and that can be cause for alarm when your office is on the top floor and so is the Bishop's office. It was several hours before we could get a service man and solve the problem but when the elevator began to operate properly we were shocked to discover that the Bishop was caught in the elevator all of that time. I thought surely that I would be "excommunicated" or at least transferred to our smallest parish, but the Bishop came out "mildly amused". A good sense of humor is an essential ingredient for ministry, no matter where we are serving. In spite of our best efforts there are moments when we wish we were somewhere else! This was one of them.

Working at the foundation was an opportunity to work closer with conference leadership, namely; the Bishop and District Superintendents, plus national leadership in stewardship. It was a role that local pastors do not have the opportunity to experience in the same way and thus my understanding of the mission of the total church was expanded. I was even more convinced that we needed to have an outreach which reached beyond the local church in order to truly do the work of the Kingdom. It also helped me realize that Christian stewardship (even the development of financial resources) is vital to the church's mission and in seeking new converts.

CHAPTER 12
The Last Hurrah!

As I was completing my 6th year in foundation work, a call came that made me evaluate where I was and to whom I should devote my last years before retirement. It was a call from a good friend who was asking me to consider leadership in a foundation which fostered support for senior citizens! I had come to Wisconsin to be a youth director (I was 26). Should I complete my years in ministry by working with and for senior adults? (I was now 61). This senior adult community was originated by my denomination and it was located in a city where I was once a pastor; and maybe most important of all, my mother had been a resident there for 16 years. My strong sense of family began to kick in and I also remembered that this retirement home cared for her all that time for a pittance of financial support. After considerable thought and prayer, Eleanor and I decided that it was the right decision and I accepted the invitation to become President and CEO of the Manor Park Foundation in West Allis, WI. Now for the first time in my ministry I was no longer directly under the supervision of a Bishop---and frankly, I missed that tie! I felt a little guilty at first; but, that didn't last long! It was the right time for me to work with a senior citizen community because now, I, too, was a senior citizen. My responsibility now had a much narrower focus and I wondered if I would be comfortable working basically with senior adults instead of leading youth groups and seeking to find new members. I was looking for gifts and financial support to keep senior adults secure in their later years. I never dreamed that could be so fulfilling, nor did I imagine it would be possible to find so many dollars for the support of senior adults. To ask for money didn't seem to be very appealing and how could that be called "Ministry"? I soon learned how wrong I was! Let me offer this one experience as an example of meaningful ministry among senior citizens: Mr. and Mrs. Andrew Olsen lived at the Village at Manor Park so I called in their home just as I might have done had I been the pastor of a local church. We had many enjoyable visits and "Andy" was forever telling how he went about "investing". I listened because I was learning. One day I stopped to visit, only to find that his wife was now in the Nursing home and within a few weeks passed away! Andrew lived by himself for several more years and I continued to visit with regularity. He provided regular but small gifts to the Foundation. One day I came to visit and Andrew wasn't there and I discovered he had been moved to the Nursing Home! I visited him there with regularity but one day I came and he was sitting on a chair in a corner, facing the wall. I asked what was wrong and he said, "I am 88 years old and I am good for nothing. I can't do anything useful for anyone anymore." That alarmed me because I knew what a good person he was. I pondered his situation for a few days, conferred with several other leaders in the retirement community and then returned to make this proposal: He was still very depressed. I said, "Andrew, I would like to make a shocking proposal. I know that you do not have any family and I know you care very much about your community so----I am here to ask you if you would consider the first gift to build a rehabilitation center that would help people in this community who remain in their homes and those who live here at the Village-----and----we need at least $500,000.00 to start! He politely thanked me and said "I will think about it"! About a week later his lawyer called to say " Mr. Olsen would like for you to come back to see him"! It didn't take me long to get there! When I arrived he said, "I thank you for thinking that I am capable of making such a gift! I won't offer you a half million dollars but I will give you $600,000.00." Eventually he gave one million dollars. As the rehab center was being constructed a nurse would push his wheel chair around the project every day and he was so pleased. But when the dedication day came Andy was too sick and frail to come and just as we were starting the dedication service his lawyer asked if he could say a few words on behalf of Mr. Olsen. This is what he said, "I am here today on behalf of Mr. Andrew Olsen. He has asked me first of all, to thank Earl Lindsay (that is me) for the greatest opportunity of his life time"! His marvelous gift provided a tremendous boost to the community and at the same time it helped him know until his last days that "he wasn't good for nothing!" Today this healing center is a lasting tribute to Andrew and Viola Olsen. It made a person know that they had worth, it blessed the senior citizens in the West Allis community and believe you me, I knew I was still in ministry!

CHAPTER 13

Changing Lanes—When One Retires And Retires And Retires!

The experience of retirement sneaked up on me! Oh, I had been preparing for nearly 10 years by building our dream home and making financial plans but emotionally I wasn't really prepared to hear "You are nearly 65 and it is time to change lanes" I mean retire? Since I was a teen ager my "burning goal" was to be a pastor. Yes, I did other things in these 46 years but I wasn't really ready for retirement. Perhaps most haunting for me was, "Can you retire from a calling? A job—yes; a profession---yes; but how do you stop doing what you believe God called you to do?

That struggle to understand who we are and what is the main purpose of our life goes on, even into our retirement years. I more clearly understand now what Dietrich Bonhoeffer was experiencing when until within a month of his death he was still asking, "who am I? Is something within me still like a beaten army fleeing in disorder from victories already achieved"?

How do you give up with a short parting ceremony what you worked so hard to obtain. Life for so long was out before you and now you are a "has been". Bishop H. Clifford Northcott, who ordained me, in his retirement years captured reality very well when he remarked, "It isn't very far from a listing in "who's who" to the questions of those who ask, "Who's that"?

I hadn't realized how much of my sense of personal worth and authority was derived from my work. One finds one's self re-examining their faith to see if you have given too much of your ambition and effort to professionalism and not enough to personal faith growth!

Yes, I had played out my options as a full time pastor and now I was a free agent! BUT with prayer and openness one's spirit begins to heal and then you realize: I have not left the ministry, I have only changed lanes---and new ministries began to appear! Susan Abraham, writing in the 2009 summer edition of the Harvard Divinity Journal says, "Our primary job in this world is to pass on life—enhanced—to future generations", and one isn't retired very long until they realize that in our retirement years we still have multiple opportunities "to pass on life—enhanced—to future generations!" In fact one can contribute both to faith issues and in other areas of life in even more unique ways. For this pastor the opportunity to do part time ministry came quicker than he had expected and in such diverse ways and places. First as a Hospice Chaplain (5 ½ years) then as a College fundraiser (5 years- travelling all over the U.S.A.) and finally as the organizer of two foundations (both to provide funds to support church and humanitarian causes). I have been an interim pastor in three different parishes and multiple opportunities to preach, counsel, marry and conduct funerals. My first Interim Pastorate (Brillion, WI) was only for 2 ½ months. I served this congregation until they could find a new pastor. They were a divided congregation who were very discouraged by all they had been through. I began by visiting in their homes, calling in the hospitals, and organizing a confirmation class. I found strong laity support and the result was much improved attendance. The sad part of this experience was my doctor's discovery of prostate cancer in my body and I had to go into immediate surgery.

The second interim pastorate (Greenville, WI) was a summer fill-in for a pastor who took a Sabbatical leave for rest and study. Both of these churches exposed me to new styles of worship and I learned in a fresh way that "you can teach old dogs new tricks". At Greenville we commuted about 115 miles each way from our home and so for the 15 week ends we stayed in the home of a different parishioner every week end. It proved to be a quick way of getting acquainted and by the end of our time we could call nearly everyone in the church by name.

The third interim pastorate, Oshkosh First United Methodist, was for 4 months. It was a larger city church where the pastor had been removed. This meant many hard feelings and the congregation was very divided with some supporting the former pastor and some outraged at what he had been accused of doing. Many members were not only disillusioned with the local church, they were angry with the denomination for what they perceived as unwilling to help solve the problem. We moved into the community and made ourselves available on a 24 hour basis. We made sure that they knew we cared deeply about them and so again we went house to house in visitation of the congregation. It was heart warming to see nearly twice as many in church as we left the congregation versus when we arrived. When there is tension in a congregation there is no better way to heal wounds and build bridges than a visit in the home of the troubled. These interim pastorates were very fulfilling experiences. So ministry continues, but at a slower pace----a pace that matches our physical pace. Life seems to move us along, so one experience seems to prepare us for the next step in life!

CHAPTER 14
Retirement---Again And Again!

Someone once said that retirement has three steps: There are the "Go-go years". That is the first period of your retirement when you try to go everywhere you hadn't been, see everything you haven't seen----it is the first 10 years of retirement. Then comes the second stage of retirement and that is called the "Slow-go years". In this 10 plus years of your retirement you don't travel as much but stay involved. And then comes the "No-go years". That is the 10 or how many years you get when you basically stay at home and let the world come to you.

After 16 years of retirement, living in the home that we designed and had built for retirement in beautiful Door County, WI, enjoying the sand beaches of Lake Michigan as our back yard and all the other cultural and scenic parts of the area, we needed to face up to a new decision. We were moving into the second stage of retirement. The aging process, the distance from medical services and the care of our little paradise started to be an issue and so we did what we never thought we would do: we placed a "For Sale" sign on our home and applied for an apartment in a retirement village! Again, at first, it seemed like we were "giving up"---but again, it was facing up to who we were and where on the "ladder of life" we were standing. We consulted first with our four children and grandchildren! The Grandchildren who had known our home as a vacation spot didn't like the idea but all four of our children said, "it's the right move". Our second son, Paul (and he reflected the response of all four) when he said, "we have lived in many houses in our time at home (in parsonages, that is) so wherever you and mother are located, that is home to us!" We didn't need anyone else's persuasion to do what we knew we should do. Now we weren't standing behind our family as we had always tried to do: they were standing behind us. Now, we were no longer looking after our children, they were looking after us. We are now located in our comfortable apartment at The Village at Manor Park, which is near 3 of our 4 children and enjoying the security of "life care". It is also where I had been the President of their Foundation (Manor Park Foundation) when I retired and near the center of the area where I had served as a pastor----and now as a resident of this Village rather than an employee, the opportunity for Christian service keeps coming. I have been asked to be a Consultant for the Village---I am leading stewardship work at the church where I once was the senior pastor; I can still comfort and counsel so many who I have known from earlier times.

Yes, as this Journey in ministry keeps extending and adjusting to who I am and what I am, the words of the Psalmist tells our story: "the Lord is our Shepherd, we do not want"! Identity theft is a popular form of stealing in our society today but in this journey through life, the forces of evil have been fierce but they could not steal the identity of a child of God! The flesh may be a little weaker but the spirit is still willing and---The trumpet still sounds"!

CHAPTER 15
And---In Conclusion

I owe so much to the church! The Church helped me find my identity, it encouraged me through scholarships, and loving friends. It provided for me employment, the opportunity to grow in faith, and always in my understanding of the world around me. The church as a world-wide institution has made possible so many acts of compassion and service that I, as an individual could never do, but from a life time of service in that world-wide church, it is my strong conviction that it is in the local congregation where it all begins. If that local church dies, the world-wide church is seriously wounded!

William H. Willimon, who is now the United Methodist Bishop of the North Alabama Conference, in one of his earlier books ('What's Right with the Church'- page 13) says it best: "the church is far richer than our individual experiences of it and more complex than any one New Testament ecclesial image. But this does not mean simply that the sum is greater than its parts. Your local congregation does not merely belong to the church; your local church is the church. It is not merely a cell of the larger organism but a manifestation of the whole organism. This suggests that the way to learn about the whole church is to look carefully at individual churches, all the while acknowledging that individual congregations do not exhaust the richness of the church universal. These congregations become rallying points for the universal church, centers for the never-ending process of congregating in the name of Jesus."

When the most prominent theologian of the neo-orthodox movement, Karl Barth, in his later years, was asked what his favorite hymn was, he replied without hesitation, "Jesus Loves Me, This I know, for the Bible tells me so"! He was familiar with and had enjoyed all of the great music of the prominent German composers, but from a life time of great music, Karl Barth, that giant among German theologians returned to his childhood to re-coop a simple song that stated clearly the heart of his beliefs; "Jesus Loves Me, this I know, for the Bible tells me so".

And, SO, I too, return to the beginning of my faith journey to claim a truth that has again and again brought light and joy to this Incredible Journey; it is a little chorus that I learned as a child and sang again and again with my brother and four sisters and then I sang it with my first granddaughter, Amy, as we drove back and forth to Door County, WI. It simply said, "This Little Light of Mine, I'm going to let it shine, let it shine, let it shine; let it shine!" He, (Jesus) provided the light and I let it shine! What a joyful and fulfilling journey it has been!

Preaching----Sharing The Words Of Life

Somewhere I read about the layman sitting next to his wife in church, listening to his pastor deliver a sermon with great emotion. He turned to his wife and said, "I wish that I had a way to unleash my frustrations like that"!

Preaching must do more than release the preacher's frustrations! A preacher needs to enter into the struggles of his congregation with a Biblical response, a compassionate spirit and a practical understanding of their circumstances. Preaching needs to be fortified by a genuine spirituality, a little humor and some hours of preparation. At least for me, the Lord never let the word "flow from my mouth" until I had considered the circumstances of the people, the changing world in which we live and the Biblical materials that were relevant.

The following six sermons are intended to speak to some of the frustrations that happen in the life of a congregation.

How does one gain respect?

Do you compromise?

IS COMPROMISE CHRISTIAN?

Scripture: Genesis 32:24-32 Romans 12:1-2

Today, I would like to put my finger on what most of us want most! It would not be riches, as helpful as that may be, it is not just success, as sweet as that sounds. It would be RESPECT! From the youth who says, "you never listen to me" to the senior citizen who laments, "I'm forgotten," the desire is not for advantage, but for respect. The problem comes for many of us in how we go about trying to get respect. The temptation is to use any shortcut that looks like it would bring us respect quickly. The Old Testament lesson today is the story of one man's search for respect---his fierce struggle to be somebody. If I were to choose one person out of popular television heroes to symbolize this man Jacob, it would be J.R. Ewing (his popularity has now faded), who was on that night soap opera called "Dallas". J.R. Ewing had a talent for deception and somehow always seemed to profit from it. Jacob knew how to profit from his manipulating and from his deception. He learned the weaknesses of others and just when to make his move.

Jacob had out-traded his brothers, he was able to cheat his father-in-law until, yes, he had become a rich man! The status symbol for Jacob was not big cars or an elaborate home, but big flocks. He even had physical strength and attractiveness. People thought of Jacob as an attractive personality. It would seem that everything was on his side. You might say he was a very successful man.

But, he had no respect. When he was alone he couldn't stand himself! Jacob had to live with Jacob…and there was his problem. He couldn't "con" God! Jacob's approach to getting what he wanted was COMPROMISE. You give up something in order to get something more important and you make sure that what you give away isn't as valuable as what you receive. Is that the way it is in the world of reality? To Jacob, the question of what is fair or what is honest was unimportant. Everyone knew he was a good trader, but no one thought of him as a good person. So much and yet so little----a host of advantages, but no respect. Is compromise wrong? To answer that question, I need to ask a question. Yes, some of you are saying, that's the way clergy give answers. They simply ask another question. But I would like to ask a question to answer a question. My question is "What are we compromising?"

Our first question of compromise should be "Is our desire for compromise a desire for advantage or a desire for the truth?" Jacob loved advantage more than integrity. In relating to his brother Esau he attempted to take his rights away. The rights of his brother had no reason to be preserved as far as Jacob was concerned. In relating to his father, he was deceptive. He knew that his father's blindness would allow him to be tricked. The world soon recognizes those who seek advantage and those who have integrity. Several years ago, two youth came to ask about marriage. It was an occasion that seemed so very joyous. The young man explained that his fiancée was Roman Catholic and very faithful and devout in her church. But, according to his explanation, he could not accept that tradition, and, therefore, they wanted to be married in our congregation. She explained that her love for him was strong and since that was his feeling it was okay with her. So they were married in our congregation. It wasn't long before I noticed the young woman coming faithfully to worship and sharing in the life of the church, but the young man was not present at all. Now it seemed to me here was a person who said he had a deep conviction about integrity, but really had only a desire for dominance.

A desire for advantage, not a desire for the truth. That is not conviction, it is plain stubbornness. My question about compromise is "Is compromise a desire for advantage, or a desire for the truth?"

The second question I have of compromise is: "Is it for the advantage of humanity or to save our own skin?" Jacob was so anxious to take care of number one that even number one couldn't stand him! But is there a time when compromise is meant to bless the world instead of curse the world? To help others instead of ourselves? I can't explain that kind of compromise but I can illustrate it. Dietrich Bonhoeffer, the German theologian, was hanged at the end of World War II by the Nazis because he had participated in a plot to kill Hitler. He believed that this was more Christian than to let the madness of Nazism continue. Now, is that a compromise? Yes, of course, it is a very serious compromise with the principles of Christianity. But not a compromise for his advantage. It was a compromise for the advantage of humanity. A compromise that created respect rather than destroying it.

The best example of compromise that I know is demonstrated by God himself! It's called forgiveness! Forgiveness is God's compromise with us. Common sense tells us that we will reap what we sow. The Old Testament says, "An eye for an eye, and a tooth for a tooth." Even Jacob believed that now he was going to get what he deserved. But God forgave him and then his family could trust him too. Forgiveness is a compromise, it isn't deserved, but it is what made Jesus the most revered person in history. His compromise was for the advantage of others and not just for his own advantage. Forgiveness is that compromise which breaks the endless chain of getting even. If you are asking, "What would God have me to do?" remember what God himself has done.

Jacob did find the peace of God. How wonderful that is! That's the good news, someone so undeserving could have the peace of God, but not until he was willing to compromise with his advantages rather than with his disadvantages. Paul Tillich used to say, "We need to do the truth, not just tell the truth." For Jacob, that began with the divine/human encounter. The Scripture describes it as a "wrestling match." It is always a wrestling match within our own spirit when we seek to be sincere and honest about the divine presence in our lives. That's where it begins for us, even as it began for Jacob.

Sydney Harris, a news commentator, tells of going to the newsstand with a Quaker friend; the friend purchased a paper and thanked the newsboy. The newsboy didn't acknowledge his thanks in any way. Mr. Harris commented, "He's a sullen fellow, isn't he?" His Quaker friend responded, "Oh, he's that way all the time". Mr. Harris then said, "Why do you continue to be so polite to him?" His friend said, "Why not? Why should I let him decide how I am going to act"" You see, the old Quaker had found a truth that was truer than the saying, "You reap what you sow". He had found a power more helpful than simply getting even. He had experienced the power of God's forgiveness and that is the compromise for the advantage of all. It was a truth that was truer than reaping what we sow---that he wouldn't compromise with anyone---and it earned him respect.

DEALING WITH DEPRESSION

GOD --- ON LIFE'S RAGGED EDGES!

Scripture: Psalm 147:1-12
Verse 3 "It is He who heals the broken in spirit."
II Corinthians 4-12
Verse 8 "Hard pressed on every side, we are never hemmed in; bewildered, we are never at wit's end; hunted, we are never abandoned."

When is the last time that you had the blues?---when your life seemed to lose its excitement---when everything put together seemed to overwhelm you? It's been a rough winter here in the north-- the fuel bills are up – and in the gloom of a winter season the waves of inferiority and feelings of failure seem to well up within us, we have come to call it "the blues". Now, it may seem to happen with some regularity in your life, perhaps even more often than you think it should; but I have news for you, you are normal! "The blues" is a time when the pieces of our life won't fit together, and that's painful! I would like to refer to these experiences as "life's ragged edges". Maybe it's a phone call and after you say a jolly "Hello!" the voice says, "Mr. Smith, this is the Internal Revenue Department, and we would like to have you come in and see us!" Maybe it is a letter from your employer and you tear open the letter to read, "Dear Mrs. Jones, due to severe reverses in business it will be necessary to terminate your employment." It ignites panic within your feelings. Maybe it's a letter from a special friend, and it begins,

"Dear John, I hate to write this letter because you are such a fine person but…." And you know the rest. It stimulates feelings of inferiority and they bubble over in your outlook on life. It's the blues! It could even be a retiree who once wondered if she would live long enough to enjoy social security - and now she wonders if the social security will last as long as she does! Yes, insecurity can grow. "The blues", they could even be triggered by a trip to the supermarket in our society. After passing through the meat department you now know what a golden calf looks like! The words of the Prophet Haggai are right up-to-date when he says in Chapter Six, "Your wages are put in a purse with holes in it." Even at the grocery store, we can be unraveled.

I have learned to refrain from judgment on what is or what is not a serious problem in other's people's lives. I remember the student who received a "B" among all of his "A"s and went to the window of his high towered dormitory, jumped out, and committed suicide. It simply drove him over the edge. Did you know that the second highest reason for death among students is suicide? Remember, what looks insignificant when past, may look insurmountable in the present. These pressures and fears – they make our lives into ragged edges – pieces that don't fit together, and then we have the blues. What can we stand on when life serves us hurt? And the pieces don't seem to fit together! Paul, in the Bible was really kicked around, and yet he writes, "I am hard pressed on every side but never hemmed in, bewildered, but never at wit's end; hunted, but never abandoned." What resources can we call on to lift us out of despair – inwardly renew us Let me point at three experiences that can rescue us from the blues and "renew a right spirit within us".

The first step away from the blues for many of us is to realize God's presence in our lives. Then, you are not alone!

The Psalmist says "it is He who heals the broken in spirit". The Scriptures are telling us that faith provides a partner, and then we are not alone. Victor Frankl spent years studying the people who had to live in concentration camps. He discovered that those who survived were not necessarily the physical strong but those who had a purpose for going on. A feeling they were not alone! Some of our old gospel hymns are not necessarily great music, but they teach us a lot of what the Scripture has said to us, for we sing "And He walks with me, and He talks with me". That old gospel hymn is saying that we have a partner if we are asking for help and believing in God's presence for our lives. So, why not experiment? Let's try making a covenant with God – and call on Him daily – and see what it does for our depression. Harvey Cox has written, "Hope isn't just optimism – hope is when our faith is in God as the final power that makes our existence meaningful." Yes, as Paul said, "Hard pressed on every side, but never hemmed in; bewildered but never at wit's end."

A second step that leads on and up from the blues is, we need love enough to live with imperfection. Jean Paul Sartre, French philosopher, once said "Hell is other people." I understand that feeling! And some of you, particularly you who are teachers, must understand it as well. We like to judge others by what we actually see, but we expect others to judge us by our good intentions. We thought that education, the refinement of our skills, would increase our understanding of each other, but you can teach a person nine languages and they can lie in all nine of them. It takes more than simply the refinement of our skills to deal with our spirit. There are "splits and gaps" in every one of us, and living with this imperfection requires a love that is motivated by more than reason. Paul said, "Bewildered, but we are never at wit's end". I am not sure all of us can say that. But he was saying that all of us need a love that can live with imperfection. I am reminded of the little girl's prayer who said, "Dear Lord, please make all of the bad people good, and all of the good people nice". It's love enough to live with imperfection – yours and mine. The gospel offers it to all of us.

The third step that leads on and up from the blues – it's courage enough to reach out instead of pull back. I'm reminded of the bulletin board notice that was on a professor's door at the University of Wisconsin in Madison. Evidently a word had been left out, but the sign said, "Due to a lack of interest, tomorrow has been cancelled". Now, that's what happens to so many of us. We pull away and hide; we cancel our tomorrow rather than reach out. The late Paul Tillich often spoke of the "courage to be". The "courage to be", I mean – reach out instead of pull back; that truly is courage. Reach out, talk to someone about your faith as well as your problems. Isolation is one of the major sources of depression today. So, call some one – call your friends – call your pastor –even call your enemies and talk about your faith as well as your problems. You will discover that it helps to hold both of you together. Paul says, "We are never abandoned to our fate". The King James Version says, "We may be cast down, but not destroyed". The Spirit of Jesus keeps us from looking for a way out and helps us find a way through. "It is He who heals the broken spirit".

Yes, there are ragged edges for all of us and certainly there are many of them in our society today. Some time ago I read about a new puzzle that is being produced for our society today. It seems that the puzzle comes with a piece missing. The purpose of the puzzle is to prepare us for life as it is today. Again and again, the very piece that we had wanted, and needed, seemed to be missing from our grasp. Is there truly a piece missing in our life? Perhaps we have lost faith to believe that God is present in our lives, and enough love to live with imperfection. Perhaps we've lost the courage to be, the courage to reach out instead of simply pull back from the hurts around us. Yes, for many, life is a puzzle with a piece missing, but often the piece that is missing is the "peace" of God--- and that is yours for the asking!

INDECISION

How Do You Make Up Your Mind?

"WHEN YOU CAN'T MAKE UP YOUR MIND!'

Scripture: Isaiah 49:8-13
Verse 11: "I will make every hill a path and build embankments for my highways."
Verse 24: "No person can serve two masters."
Verse 34: "So do not be anxious about tomorrow; each day has troubles of its own."

A popular periodical reports on a whole series of job openings! I am aware that many of you who come to worship are concerned for jobs. They are hard to find. But across the United States there are three hundred openings for one particular position; the position is college president. Now the salary is considerably above welfare rates, and the job provides plenty of thrills for the ego, and there is no lack of applicants. The reason there are so many openings is that the average length of time for a college president to stay in office is less than five years. Most college presidents are not fired; most of them resign! Why? Why? It's the battering pressure of decision-making. They get worn out making up their mind.

Most of us waste a lot of life because we make decisions three times---we worry about them before we act; we worry about them while we are making this decision; and we worry wondering if we did the right thing. Do you ever have trouble making decisions because you can't make up your mind?

It isn't always a great big decision about some tantalizing evil versus some burdensome right. For me it might be a tension between "Do I finish the bulletin when the church secretary is waiting for it again, or do I go to the hospital to see a seriously ill person who has called for me to come? Do I finish my sermon or answer the eight telephone calls on my desk?" Neither task is wrong; all of them are right. But often one must decide which one to do first and that's the painful decision-- and that's where the anxiety sets in for many of us.

Now Jesus puts it to us in Matthew's Gospel. He says, "Do not be anxious about tomorrow." He says, "Look at the birds; they have no scholarships, no savings, no pensions, no food stamps, and no welfare. Yet they go through a winter and come out singing in the spring." But you say that is not the way our world operates. The birds have no exams to pass, no production quotas to meet, no mortgages to pay, and no change of fashions to worry about. They wear the same old feathers most of the year. The Greek word for "anxious" is "to divide" and that's what anxiety does to us. It divides us and makes one part of us work against the other. I believe that more anxiety comes from indecision than from fear or from inferiority or from any known sin. We are often anxious because we can't make up our minds, and so we stand at the crossroads. We are paralyzed, unable to accomplish much of anything, and thus we waste God's greatest gift. What a waste of you and me! Jesus also said in our Scriptures today, "You cannot serve two masters." That's often where our anxiety starts! We are trying to please everybody, run in all directions, and we end up in a cocoon of anxiety...not even pleasing ourselves. Where is the contentment and the feeling of "all is right with the world" that Jesus seemed to have and offer to all of us? How do we handle that anxiousness that grips most of us at one time or another? When you can't make up your mind and feel torn apart within, I would like to suggest that you try these five steps as you seek to deal with the anxiousness of your life:

1. Let the buck stop in front of you! Let the Spirit speak to you. Don't blame everyone else for your tension. (Your kids, your parents, your job.) You can't do everything but you can do something! You can let the Spirit speak to you. We need to decide who has the last word in our lives and we often allow many masters to have that last word. But the Scripture points for us to our Lord as our first source of authority. Harvey Cox, a professor at Harvard University, says that so many of die in the waiting room. We are always waiting for someone else to make our important decisions. God wants to help you make that decision. The temptation for many of us is to blame someone else for the frustrations of our life, but I believe the first step in dealing with our anxiousness is to remember that God really wants to deal person to person with you.
2. The second step in dealing with our anxiousness is to examine our ego. Are you so anxious to be somebody that your ego is tripping you up? Inflating your importance and allowing you to rise to the level of your incompetence. The person who continuously suppresses what they feel is right, for popularity or price, is going to be anxious and hostile. This anxiousness can leave you angry at yourself and quite unlovable to others. So, examine your ego on the way to seeking peace.
3. Decide your priorities. Jesus said, "You cannot serve two masters." And we are often trying to

serve three or four. I have one son who is always telling me how rich he is going to be. That's okay, but I do hope that he will ask the questions "why" and "how". Will we sacrifice friendships and the trust of others in order to be rich? We might avoid being a burden on society because financially we can care for ourselves, but in the process we can become a bore to society. Can you feel good about what you're doing? I'd like my son and other sons and daughters to ask themselves that question before they settle simply for riches. Are you making the world any better place than you found it? Or will you be a leech on society and thus feel like a worm? I have recently returned from Korea and so I am conscious of Americans who have had a part in providing freedom for South Koreans. The story is told of General Dean who commanded the American forces during the Korean War and at one time was captured by the North Koreans. He was told that he was about to be put to death and that he could write a note to his family. In the note, General Dean said to his son, "Dear son, remember the word is not riches, or popularity, or fame; the word is integrity." Priorities drive away our anxiousness and create wholeness. How important it is to remember "the word is integrity".

4. Take one day at a time. The last verse of our Scriptures today in the New Testament says, "Each day has troubles enough of its own." That's sort of a negative way of expressing it, but I believe that it's saying, "Don't borrow trouble from tomorrow." I have carried a little black book in my pocket for fifty three years of ministry. I have a little book for each year of that

time, and each year it seems to be fuller and fuller. I must confess to you that I sometimes do not look very far ahead in it because if I were to allow all the things written in there to focus in my mind at once, I would feel overwhelmed. I try not to borrow trouble from tomorrow. It is an important step in dealing with anxiousness. A respected doctor made a study of his patients that seemed to be suffering from anxiety. He discovered that forty percent were disturbed over things that never happened. Thirty percent were anxious over things of the past that could no longer be changed. Twelve percent were suffering from pure imagination in this area. Ten percent were suffering over other people's problems. Only eight percent of his patients had real personal problems that merited anxiousness. I'm saying, "Don't borrow trouble from tomorrow". Pray about it and lay it down. Seek God's help with today, and tomorrow won't be so hard to handle.

5. Reach out and touch somebody! Some of you read about the twelve year old boy who died recently but lived for all of his years in a bubble. This young man could not be touched or could not touch anyone. What a way to live, and yet many of us try living like that much of the time. Consider another doctor's approach to healing. This doctor asked his patients to pray for each other. One person who had an allergy was asked to pray for another who had cancer. A patient who had broken bones was asked to pray for another who had emotional pressures. The result of this relationship was that anxiety dropped immensely in all of the patients. Their concern being directed outward, instead of

> inward, made a new emotional relationship for their life. They felt a part of healing instead a part of sickness. When you are filled with anxiety and feelings of worthlessness, reach out and touch somebody—and guess who gets healed!

When you are paralyzed by anxiousness, no matter what reason you offer, consider these steps that could lead you on:

1. Let the buck stop in front of you.
2. Examine your ego.
3. Examine your priorities.
4. Take one day at a time.
5. Reach out and touch someone else's need.

Jesus says, "Oh, ye of little faith". That is often us, and that is where we start but that is not where we need end the story. Sometime ago I read about a ten year old boy who was explaining to his friend how his mother had brought home a new baby sister. He said that his mother, along with a number of mothers, were in the hospital and that since his mother was the first one to go home, she went to the window of the nursery and chose the most beautiful and the best child to take home with her. Then he went on to say that the next mother to go home could choose the second best, and the third mother the third best, until all of the mothers had gone home and the children were taken with them. Now if that is the way children are chosen in the maternity ward or claimed to be taken home, many of us would still be in the maternity ward. But God doesn't relate that way. God relates to us as those mothers related to their child. They knew which one was theirs. And that one is always the most beautiful child. So God cares for his own. He knows each one of us and knows our needs. He seeks to offer to us the strength to deal with our anxiousness. So do not let anxiousness isolate you; you need not be alone. The spirit of

Jesus Christ, can be extended to those who are anxious and in extending strength to them a life, yours and mine, can be made more useful and more wholesome.

CRISIS IN THE PASTOR'S FAMILY

SOLID ROCKS IN SLIPPERY PLACES!

I don't think that Eleanor and I are pessimistic people---but frankly, this last year had been a "sink hole" for the Lindsays! My father and mother used to tell me about "quick sand" in the swamps of northern Minnesota, and how it could pull you down and eventually suffocate you! As the year proceeded, we began to feel as if we had our feet in quick sand---and so many of our life long dreams began to fade!

I never really expected to experience this kind of circumstance---life has always been so good to us---but BANG—there was crises—like we had never experienced! We have spent a lot of our life helping the helpless—but now, we were the helpless! The message today is a fresh example of how God enters our lives, especially in times of crises! And somehow it has increased our understanding of the Almighty --- it is where we found Solid Rocks to stand on, when we were passing through Slippery Places!

For 14 years Eleanor and I have been spending our winters in AZ. That doesn't sound like crisis, and it sure beats shoveling snow, but late last March, Eleanor began complaining about a severe pain between her shoulder blades. I called the Rescue Squad, who refused to take her because she wasn't having a heart attack and we didn't have $800.00 cash to give them up front for the ride, so our good friends, David and Sharon Rumachik, transported her to Mountain Vista Hospital in Mesa.. We discovered that her kidneys had failed and for 3 weeks she remained unconscious or semi- conscious and on dialysis for 6 days! We thought that was the bottom-- but it wasn't! Staph infection attacked her heart, kidneys, lungs and settled in her spine. Our doctor and his 6 specialists said they could do no more! All 4 of our children came to see their mother and I was just numb. If we ever needed something solid to stand on it was now. We felt so helpless and so we prayed and held on to each other---we did know how to do both of those. Soon we began to hear from the churches and the many Christian friends that we had accumulated over a life time and they all said "we will be praying for you". We couldn't even have imagined the response. In the 4th week Eleanor began to respond—she started talking to us, even complaining about the food, asking about her children and grandchildren and expressing gratitude. We thought life was looking up. Eleanor's sister, Elaine, came to be with her in the hospital and so I went home to Wisconsin to care for some matters and to attend my 50th reunion of Seminary Graduation only to be involved in a horrific car accident. It snapped my big Lincoln into two pieces like a piece of peanut brittle and the jaws of life were necessary to remove me from the wreckage---so now I am in Froedtert Hospital in Milwaukee and Eleanor is in Promise Hospital in Phoenix, AZ. It was our lowest moment! I felt like Job in Biblical times—"My God 'why' have you abandoned us"? It was then that our daughter rose to the challenge: we wanted to bring Eleanor home to Wisconsin but the doctors said "only by Med-flight" and the cost was $20,000.00 and no insurance covered it. Being a Minister all of my life, I didn't have that kind of money and so our daughter negotiated with Midwest Express and with the help of the Fire Dept in Phoenix and the Sheriff's Dept. in Milwaukee she was transported by ambulance on a stretcher to the plane and then in Milwaukee to the Rehab center, which was her home for another 3 ½ months. In September, however, she moved into a small apt. with me and now she was laughing and responding, and bragging about her great grandson, complaining about my cooking and learning to walk all over again. What a transformation! What a miracle!

Now, I am sharing this traumatic experience because in our lowest moments, when it seemed that 57 years together was about to end, we found some Solid Rocks that held us above destruction and returned us to the joy of life---even in such Slippery Places!

The first Rock that held us up and held us together was our family. They really showed up! With their love and compassion, with their presence, and with their resources! One son came twice and then later sent his credit card. Another son flew out twice and then drove our car back to Wisconsin, our oldest son also flew out to see his mom, our only daughter came early on and stayed until her mom regained consciousness and then came back to fly home with her. For years their hands had been in my billfold, but now my hand was in theirs and with their urging! When Eleanor arrived in Milwaukee at the airport, all the kids and grandkids were at the airport to meet her. What a reunion that was!!

The Scriptures say "train a child in the ways of the Lord and they will not depart from it". Well, after raising 4 we haven't always been so sure of that! Once I went to court with one of my sons who was charged with driving his motorcycle 86 miles an hour down main street. I was too embarrassed to call an attorney, and I knew we would lose! I am saying that clergy kids are as bad as any other kind. I am also saying that parenting begins with small children, but it continues in building relationships all of our life. I have argued with all 4 of mine, searched through the night for all 4 and sparred a few rounds with my boys. They didn't always seem to remember the ways of the Lord---and neither did we! We all had to learn "over and over" how to say "I am sorry and I love you"---even when we are grandparents. We need to let them know how proud we are of their achievements---not just when they are cute little kids---but all of their lives! And when you can't be proud of them, they still need to know "you care"---that's parenting and, when the chips are down, their faith, their values, their love and support is beyond our imagination! Yes, as we tried to crawl out of our "sink hole" there they were: " Rocks in our Slippery Places" .

The second source of power that worked for us even when our feet were in quick sand: it can look so hypocritical—it can look so generic—until you really need it. It is called The Christian Community. Our brothers and sisters in the Lord! When Saul, who became Paul, found the Christian Faith as he traveled on the road to Damascus and was brought into the city—defenseless—suffering from a sun stroke, his enemies wanted to destroy him and the Christians were afraid of a person who had been persecuting them, but when he professed his faith—at the risk of their lives, they gathered and let him down over the city wall in a basket and saved his life. That is the Christian Community. In the last few months, I have felt something in common with Saul, or Paul, because we have had so much love and support from the Christian Community. Eleanor and I have lived in many communities: some were small and rural, others were large and important cities, BUT, during this crisis time in our lives we have heard from everyone of them—from children and youth, from people I married and people whose parents I buried, from Catholics, Protestants, Jews, from Bishops and College Presidents and factory workers---from all of them came cards, visits, and phone calls---all of them saying, "We are praying for you". The support of the Christian Community has been overwhelming! I haven't always felt good about the Christian Community---even in my own denomination I question so many decisions BUT he or she who leaves the church out of their life has lost a Rock that can rise up to sustain them in life's Slippery Places!

The final Rock that is there for us in our times of great need—I knew it was there—I've used it before—BUT, this time—this time, it was so clear: It was the POWER OF PRAYER—something I can't explain, something I can't control. In our gospel lesson today, we meet Peter, trying to walk on water! All of us in our youthful days have tried that---just sure that we can handle anything. We have to admire Peter's self confidence but not his faith. Why? Because he allowed his fears of the waves to control him instead of his faith in Jesus' presence! We, too, have done that in times of crisis! But when Peter looked again to Jesus there was help and there was hope. The impossible had become possible and that is what happened to us. I have been a pastor for nearly 58 years and I believe that good preaching is essential to an alive church, and Bible study is a vital part of a growing faith BUT if I could identify the single most important spiritual power in Christianity today—it would be the Power of Prayer. Why? Because it allows other believers to reach out to us and hold up our need to the Almighty. That makes a Solid Rock for each of us when we are in Slippery Places!

There may be other answers out there but when your body is throbbing with pain and the influence and connections you have always depended on don't work, and you can see no light at the end of your tunnel, then remember these three Solid Rocks: your Family, the Christian Community and the Power of Prayer---Solid Rocks in Slippery Places! Over the years, in times of crisis, when my back was against the wall, the words of one theologian, Albert Outler, have come to me again and again: "My God doesn't call all the shots, I have called too many, But He does share all the blows". A Rock in a Slippery Place!

Scriptures for "SOLID ROCKS IN SLIPPERY PLACES"
Exodus 20:12 "Honor your father and your mother that their days may be long in the land which the Lord has given them"!
Proverbs 22:6 "Train a child in the way he should go, and when he is older, he will not depart from it"!
Maatthew 14:22-33 vs. 30 "But when he felt the wind, he was afraid, and beginning to sink, he cried out, 'Lord, save me'"
Acts 9:25 "And at night his friends led him to the city wall and let him down over the wall in a basket."

WHEN YOU REACH SENIOR STATUS

"A FAITH FOR SENIOR CITIZENS"

Scripture: Psalm 39:4-7 verse 5..."and my age is as nothing before you."
John 3:14-17 verse 16..."whosoever believes"

In recent times I have recognized something that I had never noticed at an earlier age: Jesus didn't say much about Senior Citizens! He has plenty to say about children, about the rich, the young, about the leaders of his day, the Sadducees and the Pharisees, BUT not much about senior citizens! Today I want to speak to Senior Citizens and where should be a better place?

Senior Citizens:

People, whose major career is over.

People, who have had considerable experience with life!

People, who are trying to find a new identity for their life as they claim the title "retired".

Nearly 10 years ago, my denomination held a very special service and at that service they presented to a few of us, a beautiful certificate engraved in gold with our name on it! And what it really said was "You are retired!" What a shock! Yes, I knew it was coming. But, after 45 years, I was severed from what I had been doing nearly every Sunday since I was 20 years old! I was retired---a Senior Citizen! All those years of going to school and all that experience—I was now being traded for a new recruit, who had no experience. It seemed like life was down the drain!

Does God have a place for us when we are senior citizens and retired? When we are no longer a candidate for the really important positions in society? Can we stay alive all of our life? Becoming a Senior Citizen and entering retirement may shake up our self esteem temporarily, but we soon begin to realize that God isn't limited by our best or worst years! As one comes to retirement, one needs to hear the Psalmist as in the 39th Psalm where he says, "My age is as nothing before you." That is where we start this morning! Someone once pointed out to me that there are three stages to these years called Retirement, and they are very different than our earlier years.

The First Stage is called the "Go Go Years"! We try to do everything we always wanted to do---so we go, go, go! That is where many of us are right now!

The Second Stage isn't too far behind---it is called the "Slow Go Years"! It is when arthritis and slowing energy is catching up to us.

And then there are the "No Go Years"! That is when the doctor's office and the bathroom get most of our time.

Now, how can we experience God's presence in these circumstances? Let me simply suggest to you the way many of us have found the reality of God and the love of Jesus in our senior years. First of all, we begin by trying to better understand who we are. When Deitrich Bonhoeffer, a leader of the church in Germany, was imprisoned for his Christian beliefs and his life changed from the privileged existence of a University Professor to the confinement of one small prison cell, he said "I found myself asking 'who am I anyway and what am I for'?" Those are basic questions in times of change. They are good questions when your life is changing and the road ahead doesn't have the same resources that you had known in earlier years. The Psalmist in the 39th Psalm gives us the first question to ask ourselves as we come to retirement---for in the 5th verse he asks "What is the measure of my days?" In retirement the fluff of life comes off and you are what you are ---just one of God's children!

The second step as we move into retirement is to re-examine our roots! Remember when you thought your parents didn't know very much?—And especially when it came to religion! They were so narrow and unscientific! You didn't want to be like that…but as time moved along you saw less of their faults and more of their wisdom! Retirement is a good time to re-examine your roots! Not just family history but faith history! Why did our parents suffer so many hardships and still believe in God's guidance? My family were depression farmers and there was a time when the banker delivered the stunning news! We were going to lose the farm! My parents and all of the family knelt by the kitchen chairs and began to pray. Well—they didn't lose the farm and I often think of their faith and courage! It overshadows their weaknesses. As the Psalmist says in verse 12: "We are sojourners. We are living first by faith, as our fathers and mothers were"! Where did we get our ideas of 'what is right, right for us and right for the world'?" Retirement is a good time to review our faith roots---not just our family roots. No wonder some of us sing "Faith of our fathers, living still"!

A third step on the way to a deeply meaningful faith in one's retirement years is to look around and recognize what is really needed and where you are really needed! The world has changed and you have changed but that doesn't make us helpless. We need to ask "What can I do, and what can I do best?" It is a new adventure. Robert Schuller of Crystal Cathedral Fame has an answer for all of us senior citizens, he said, "Find a need and meet it"! When I retired, I remembered that I had entered the ministry to be a youth director, but, now I am a Hospice

Chaplain. I found a need and I met it. Then I met the senior vice president of a very large trucking firm and a Medical Doctor, both of them were retired but they, too, had found a need among Hospice patients and were trying to meet it. As I retired, my original college was about to close for lack of money---so, I took on the job of raising funds. I knew an old man could do a better job than a college student at raising funds. I found a need and I tried to meet it. I joined Habitat for Humanity and helped to build homes for the homeless. Frankly, I couldn't drive a nail straight but raising funds needed to be done. You just have to hear the 39th Psalm again for in my Bible it says "My age is as nothing to you". That's the way God sees us. We are all "Children of God". Our age is as nothing to Him. As Bonnie Prudden once said,"You can't turn back the clock, but you can wind it up again!"

Finally, a Faith for Senior Citizens gets stronger and more meaningful when the senior citizen looks forward and not backward. Yes, we like to tell about great moments in our past—and that's o.k. We like to tell about the times when we were in school---times when we experienced a great accomplishment---times with our children and grandchildren. But, it is when we can help someone have a better future, that our faith begins to glow! Remember the black lady in Birmingham who was marching for civil rights and she said, "I'm not marching for myself' I am marching for my grandchildren!" That's looking forward—not backward! Moses, the senior citizen, never made it to where he was planning to go, but many others did because he was willing to start out. He was looking forward and not backward! His eye was on the future and not the past! It makes faith real for Senior Citizens. It keeps excitement in life. The late Halford Luccock at Yale once said, "The Spirit of Jesus is a well of perpetual youth. He doesn't keep our bodies from aging

BUT He keeps our spirits from molding!" So, remember in these retirement years "We haven't quit living---we have just changed lanes! For "Whosoever will, young and old, may come"!

MONEY MATTERS --- TO THE INDIVIDUAL

AND TO THE CONGREGATION

"You can take from me all of the advantages that I have enjoyed, but – no one is going to take from me the joy of giving".
My mother, Violet Mary Lindsay

YOU CAN COUNT ON ME!

Scripture: Luke 19:1-10

I would like to begin with a biblical story that I learned when I was just a child. It is a story that many of you learned as children too.

It is the story of when Zacheus met Jesus. Let us zero in on Zacheus! He was a short, crooked, rich, social outcast who climbed up in a tree so he could see Jesus pass by---I understand. At 5 ft.6 in., I too, have looked at the back of many heads and couldn't see what was happening on the playing field. But---that was not the only reason Zacheus was up a tree. No one wanted to stand next to him. He was not only short, he had also shortchanged most everyone in his community. He was a "no count" who couldn't be counted on to help anyone. His first question was always "What's in it for me?" Why would he want to see Jesus? Perhaps it was partly curiosity. After all, Jesus was well known. But even more compelling than curiosity, was the empty feeling in his life.

Lately, I have come to realize that the story of Zacheus is really for adults---the children of God. Now, I don't want to do with this story what so many have done with the Bible---read more into it than they read out of it, but, I have come to realize why so many of us remember that old Bible story. It is not just that Jesus took in a social outcast—it's that Zacheus, like so many of us, spend so much of our life, "up a tree" about something. We can't quite get life to come together. Our sources of satisfaction seem to be just a little out of our reach. Now that was the problem for Zacheus too. Zacheus had so many things going for him, but with all of his advantages they wouldn't fill the vacuum in his life. He could never quite feel good about his life. There was something missing! So, here he was---right where we often find ourselves---"up a tree"---looking for something we can't quite find!

Like Zacheus, we too have come to church---looking for the power that will put our life together. Like Zacheus, each one of us have been given so many resources, so many advantages, and yet they don't seem to produce the satisfaction, the fulfillment, we thought they would. All of us have time (sometimes more than we want), we have special talents (everyone of us can do something no one else can do) and we have more treasure, more resources, than the people in any other country of the world. Yes, we have been given time, but we never seem to quite have enough of it and at any age! Talk to a middle school student. It should be an ideal age---young enough to be a child and yet old enough to do adult things without being expected to carry much responsibility. But they will tell you they are busy. There's school and friends, and choir and more than they can get done. They don't have enough time. Ask a University student. I asked my college son, "Have you been to the college church yet?" He exploded! "I have a full load of credits, I have a job, I have Crew and I have a girl friend---I don't have time" Ask a parent. More than one young mother has yearningly said "I can't wait til these kids grow up so I can have some time to myself". Well---I have news for you. The problems change but you are a parent all of your life and time doesn't expand. Ask the retired. Don't some of you retired people who are present today, wonder how you ever had time to hold down a full time job?

You see more time didn't satisfy Zacheus. He could set his own schedule, he was a free lancer—but not until he allowed time for Jesus to come into his life did he find a sense of satisfaction. In all of his free time he felt empty. That may be our problem too! Just more time is not necessarily satisfying. After Zacheus met Jesus his life seemed to be in focus. He heard things like the cry of the needy. He actually felt compassion and now time was on his side. He now had time for the things that create satisfaction. Yes, there was Zacheus—up a tree—he had been misusing another God-given resource. His talent. Zacheus thought the way to get ahead in life was to outsmart everybody else. Be shrewd! Zacheus had a lot of talents. He was a middle man. His boss was the Romans---his customers were the Jews and he contracted to collect the taxes for a price and the Romans protected him. It was free enterprise at its worst. But, like so many of us talented people—he seemed to outsmart himself. Brilliant people consumed by greed and self-centeredness usually do. People hated Zacheus for his dishonesty and yes, he was up a tree because he hated himself. Real satisfaction doesn't come by outsmarting everyone else. Just having talent wasn't enough and so Zacheus was "up a tree"---not feeling good about his life or his world. We understand the feeling! God help us not to give so much first rate efforts to so many second rate causes!

Yes, Zacheus was "up a tree", unhappy, unreliable, really unwanted basically because of what he would do for his treasure---his money. O'Henry, the American writer of short stories, is famous for a two word statement. The statement is "money talks". My, what it said about Zacheus! My, what it says about us! You see, Zacheus knew how to get it together but, it didn't seem to get him anywhere---until he met Jesus. Jesus changed his source of satisfaction. He focused his life and then a "no count" could be counted upon. Zacheus jumped down from that tree to say "You can count on me"! and Jesus said, "Salvation has come to this house today". Then and there his money began to work for him instead of he for his money! Yes, his money had been talking about him all the time and it said "cheater, tightwad, thief, self-centered"! But when Zacheus really met Jesus and his priorities were changed, even his money helped him experience satisfaction. He even volunteered to repay those he had cheated at a rate of 4 to 1. It was fun to share, and the satisfaction began to flow. Now, the world could count on Zacheus! Now he was given respect and included by his community. You see, when the teachings of Jesus permeated Zacheus he was changed from a scalping person (one who ripped you off) to a helping person (one who offered more than he had taken). From a "no count" to a person who announced "You can count on me"! When we can't be counted on, we reduce our worth to everyone.

Now, Zacheus was no longer "up a tree" for Jesus said, "you come down out of that tree. I am coming to your house today"! He did and He will. This morning I ask you to think back in your life and identify some of the people you could always count on to care about you. Name them in your heart! Perhaps it was a Sunday School teacher or a neighbor or someone who reached out to you when you so desperately needed it, but didn't deserve it. People who said, "you can count on me". Now someone here might find fault with every name that you mention but remember, saints are not perfect---they are just people who have said to their Lord and to themselves, "You can count on me". I remember a handicapped older person who was struggling to climb the many steps to her church and I said to her "isn't there a church that is easier to get into?" She said, "No, there isn't. It is o.k. because I get a lot of love in this church"!

But now, the choice is ours---not Jesus or St. Paul, or John Wesley or our forefathers who built this church—can we be counted on to carry the future of this church? I remember when the congregation that I was serving was struggling with the question of should we build a new church. At the congregational meeting, an older man sitting in the back row stood up and said "I didn't do a thing to build this church, but, I have to realize that IT IS NOW OUR TIME IN GOD'S PLAN". The future of this church is in our hands. In the years ahead, if this church is to be a vital Christian witness, it is going to be because persons of all ages have offered unto God their time, their talent and their treasures and with a deep down sense of joy, they have shouted unto their children and their grandchildren "You can count on me"! We are the link between the dreams of our forefathers and the dreams of our children. Can they count on us?

Let me close with a very personal experience. After my father's death, my mother came to live at Methodist Manor (The Village at Manor Park) in West Allis, WI. She loved it. No cleaning, no cooking, no snow to shovel, lots of friends and a great chaplain. One day, however, the Administration called to say "we want to meet with you and your mother". The problem was, she needed to move into the health center because she was physically no longer able to continue life in her comfortable apartment. The issue, however, was not the move---that was o.k.—the issue was from a life-time of living—a big family---big houses—her accumulated possessions. How do you boil down all you have accumulated in life to living in one room with someone you never met before? What now is worth keeping? For your own sake, think about that question! I had advised many people in such a moment but when it came to my own mother I was tongue-tied. Finally, my little four foot, ten inch mother rose to her full stature and announced, "I have made the decision. I will take 4 items with me into my new room. I want my bedroom slippers (not a bad choice), my New Testament and my large print Psalms (she read both of them more than the Milwaukee Journal and Newsweek Magazine) and then she hesitated----and---I also want my church offering envelopes". We were shocked. Finally I said, "Mother, you have four daughters and two sons---we can do the giving for you". At that point her Irish ancestry almost overwhelmed her Christ spirit, as she said, "You can take away from me all the things I have accumulated along the way in this life but no one, nobody is going to take away from me the Joy of Giving". It was her ultimate satisfaction. There isn't really much more to say except---no matter what your age or station in life---don't let anyone take away from you, the Joy—the fulfillment of Giving! And don't take it away from yourself. For if you can't be counted on, you haven't found the satisfaction, the joy that God has waiting for you. You see, the real miracle isn't about money: it is about the discovery of God's power for us!

An Addendum

The heart of this book is in the story of ministry as it unfolds in the preceding chapters, however from a life time of pastoral ministry this addendum identifies three critical areas of Programming and Emphasis that help to make a more vital witness of faith. The following are the three areas of concern--for pastors of the present and pastors of the future:

I. <u>**The Use of Time**</u>

I was not a very organized person---as a youth my way of cleaning my room began by scooping everything on the top of my dresser into the top drawer. It was not the best method. I had a poor beginning in the use of time. My parents were very committed Christians and we just never missed church BUT, we almost always arrived late. My mother claimed it was because it took so long to "curl" my four sister's hair!----and of course, that needed to happen before we arrived at church! We were always late---could it be because my parents were not, for whatever reason, very good at organizing their time? I brought this "handicap" to the ministry but thanks again to the good Lord, He matched me up with an organized wife!

Since my first appointment as a pastor was to three churches (a circuit) I had to learn quickly to be on time. Some times I have over compensated by speeding in an attempt to be on time and a police officer has recognized my efforts with an expensive ticket. We live and learn! The organization of time, however, is much more than arriving at the appointed time. It is discipline and it is organization of one's life. In no profession is it more necessary than in the life of a pastor. After all, we do not punch a time clock nor are we given a specific assignment to complete by a given time. In a sense we are "free agents". We must develop our own disciplines. No one else can do that for us! For me it didn't happen over night, but over time a plan began to develop that included the following: a devotional time----a study time---an organizational time---a family and recreational time.

The devotional time came first. It is a time to renew my spirit and spirits—time for prayer and Bible reading time for quietness and meditation---time to dream about the future and reminisce in the past. It is a time for composure. Without sounding too sanctimonious I want to say "we need to take time to be holy"!

A pastor needs study time---time for sermon preparation for next Sunday, next month and next year! Time to acquaint one's self with theological issues, history and also the latest news---time to read novels and children's books. I usually reserved mornings for study time.

A pastor needs organizational time. Time for pastoral calls, committee meetings, weddings, funerals and denominational involvement (this area could eat up all of your time if you allowed it to do so. It is an easy temptation to be "out of town" serving the church universal and neglect the church "in town" which isn't always as glamorous).

Weddings and funerals are some of the very best times to minister one on one. They are far more than social and cultural events. Pastors need to be, with some regularity, at board and committee meetings, both for input and for awareness----and please don't short change a pastoral call! You will learn more about that family and each person in it than anywhere else.

And---finally, a pastor needs family time and recreation time! In one parish we organized a boat club. Families brought their children (and the neighbor's kids) and it grew until there were some times nearly one hundred. We traveled on the nearby rivers and lakes, even using our vacation time to do longer river trips. It was a great family fun time and a time of bonding with our church family--for both of us (my wife and myself), and our children. Eventually, we were able to have an "up north" get-a-way cottage which contributed substantially to our emotional and spiritual health. Travel can also be great recreation and at the same time a wonderful learning experience. We experienced strong bonding with our congregation as the result of organizing travel experiences for our congregations and going with them! I am the world's worst golfer, (my sons and members of the congregations will testify to that truth,) but, they have had a good laugh and I have had some needed exercise.

SO, today I possess 57 Daily Suggester Books (which are provided by my denomination) that represent 57 years of life to prove that I have learned something about organizing my life and ministry!

II. **Money Changers in the Temple**

The second concern that troubles many pastors today is how to handle Christian Stewardship, especially the financial part of Christian Stewardship. Pastors like to avoid being involved in "money matters". They will say "that's the laymen's responsibility" and "the love of money is the root of all evil" (I Timothy 6:10).

For sixteen years I served my denomination as the Chairperson of Stewardship in the State of Wisconsin. I traveled all over our state leading 85 Stewardship programs in small, medium and large congregations. Again and again, the pastors wanted someone else to handle "financial drives". Their training, their "mind set" just did not include leadership in financial matters. There was also a real lack of interest in establishing an accountability system to protect both their congregational leaders and their own reputation. Most congregations had volunteer treasurers and the pastor wasn't interested in calling them into question. It could create tension and problems for the pastor.

This author is not intending to outline s complete program of financial stewardship but I would like to offer the following suggestions for establishing your leadership in Christian Stewardship:

1. 1. As a pastor, assume the leadership for finances and seek training from your denomination or elsewhere, for yourself and your leaders
2. Set the example with your own giving of both time and gifts. The "smallness of thinking" often begins with the pastor and the congregation follows. Pastor needs to tithe as well as laymen.
3. Remember, giving isn't just to "pay the bills". Giving is a way of life that creates a caring, emotionally and spiritually healthy person. Giving is the thermometer of our love.
4. Be sure and choose leaders from your congregation who truly believes in giving to lead your Stewardship Program---not just people with prominent names or positions in the community. A banker may be a respected leader in the community but if his giving record in church is very poor, he can't lead a church stewardship program.

If your congregation is to grow and be a caring and creative Christian Community, it will need strong leadership in stewardship and that begins with the pastor.

Last but not least, in order to establish an atmosphere of trust and integrity, make sure that all financial records in the congregation are audited yearly. If one can't afford a professional auditor, seek to trade volunteer auditors with another congregation. Financial integrity is an essential witness to your congregation and your community.

III. **Finding new disciples—the necessity for growth!**

My denomination (the United Methodist Church) seems to have lost its way! In the late 60's we reached over eleven million members to become the largest Protestant denomination in the U.S. but today (2010) we are nearer to eight million members. What happened? Perhaps it is the changing patterns in our society with so many causes competing for our time, perhaps our membership has grown older and perhaps it could be that we lack the zeal and commitment to go forth and make new disciples.

Regardless of the changes in our society the aging of our present membership, the Biblical invitation of Matthew 28:18-20 to "Go and make disciples of all nations" is still a compelling call to all Christians! Certainly in earlier years the influence of society and the aging of members took place as well. In our anxiousness to be ecumenical and inclusive we have sometimes left behind or left out the necessity of commitment. It is the pastor's responsibility and privilege to feed his/her flock and to find new sheep! No amount of salary or fringe benefits will guarantee that result. It takes a pastor's commitment and a supportive laity to create a growing and caring congregation. In the years that it was my privilege to be a local pastor, the congregations where I served, received over 2500 new members. While church membership does not necessarily mean one is a committed Christian, it does mean that each person who accepted membership in the Christian Church has stood before a congregation and publicly declared, "I confess Jesus Christ as my Savior" and I "receive and profess the Christian faith as contained in the Scriptures of the Old and New Testaments (Book of Discipline of the United Methodist Church, paragraph 217). It also means that the Church community needs to do a better job of nurturing new Christians so they can "overcome the world" rather than be overcome by the world. To reach new members and keep new members, the local church needs a plan. Perhaps the following suggestions could make difference for a pastor and a congregation:

a. Notice the children---tell them stories about Jesus, visit their classes—include them.
b. Visit the youth groups—listen to them---include them in leadership. It is a valuable time so do more than entertain them. Be honest and open---they will respond!
c. In times of crisis, be there----a death—a divorce—a hospital visit. And if you can't be there share your explanation, with compassion!
d. Pastors, be a good student of the Word so you can feed your flock!
e. Have a visual presence in the community---at a service club or PTA etc. ---and keep your congregation in the media (newspaper, radio, television).

But, someone is still asking, "In our society where privacy is so important, how or where do you find new members"? Let me count the ways!

1. First and foremost, every pastor needs to encourage their congregation to invite their neighbors and their friends! Do you know that research reveals that the majority of new members come to a church through an invitation by the laity? If a new person or family knows someone at your church they are much more liable to come.
2. When a new family visits your congregation, make a pastoral call to their home or even their place of business, within a week of their visit to church. Newcomers prefer to hear from a pastor first. Be sure to greet them, if they return.

3. After about two weeks have a layperson or persons about their age call on them. New families like to know there are people near their age in the congregation.
4. People don't attend a church because it is nearby or close to them. They will drive clear across town, if they feel you have a dynamic program. Be sure to tell them what is going on at your church and what you have for every member of the family.
5. And finally, follow up on those who are not coming after they have started----but, do not continue to pester them. Maybe you can correct some misunderstanding or by your visit, let them know you sincerely want them.

Robert Schuler, the pastor of the famous Crystal Cathedral in California, once identified what he considered to be the essential ingredient of a creative and growing church. He simply said, "a pastor and a congregation must find a need and meet it". It is the key to many a searching heart. Remember again what Jesus said to his disciples "Go therefore and make disciples of all nations, baptizing them in the name of the Father, Son, and Holy Spirit, and teaching them to obey everything that I have commanded you. And remember, I am with you always, to the end of the age". It is the ultimate motivation for Christians!

LaVergne, TN USA
27 July 2010
191069LV00004B/4/P